ANNABELLE LEVER

On
Privacy

NEW YORK AND LONDON

First published 2012
by Routledge
605 Third Avenue, New York, NY 10017
4 Park Square, Milton Park, Abingdon, Oxon OX14 4RN
Routledge is an imprint of the Taylor & Francis Group, an informa business

© 2012 Taylor & Francis

The right of Annabelle Lever to be identified as author of this work has been asserted by him/her in accordance with sections 77 and 78 of the Copyright, Designs and Patents Act 1988.

All rights reserved. No part of this book may be reprinted or reproduced or utilized in any form or by any electronic, mechanical, or other means, now known or hereafter invented, including photocopying and recording, or in any information storage or retrieval system, without permission in writing from the publishers.

Trademark notice: Product or corporate names may be trademarks or registered trademarks, and are used only for identification and explanation without intent to infringe.

Library of Congress Cataloging in Publication Data
Lever, Annabelle.
  On privacy/Annabelle Lever.—1st ed.
  p. cm.—(Thinking in action)
  1. Privacy, Right of. I. Title.
  JC596.L49 2011
  323.44'8—dc23   2011023585

ISBN: 978-0-415-39569-4 (hbk)
ISBN: 978-0-415-39570-0 (pbk)
ISBN: 978-0-203-15666-7 (ebk)

Typeset in Joanna and DIN
by Florence Production Ltd, Stoodleigh, Devon

On
Privacy

This book explores the Janus-faced features of privacy, and looks at their implications for the control of personal information, for sexual and reproductive freedom, and for democratic politics. It asks what, if anything, is wrong with asking women to get licenses in order to have children, given that pregnancy and childbirth can seriously damage your health. It considers whether employers should be able to monitor the friendships and financial affairs of employees, and whether we are entitled to know whenever someone rich, famous, or powerful has cancer, or an adulterous affair. It considers whether we are entitled to privacy in public and, if so, what this might mean for the use of CCTV cameras, the treatment of the homeless, and the provision of public facilities such as parks, libraries, and lavatories.

Above all, the book seeks to understand whether and, if so, why privacy is valuable in a democratic society, and what implications privacy has for the ways we see and treat each other. The ideas about privacy we have inherited from the past are marked by beliefs about what is desirable, realistic, and possible which predate democratic government and, in some cases, predate constitutional government as well. Hence, this book argues, although privacy is an important democratic value, we can only realize that value if we use democratic ideas about the freedom, equality, security, and rights of individuals to guide our understanding of privacy.

Annabelle Lever is Associate Professor of Normative Political Theory at the University of Geneva in Switzerland.

Praise for the series

'. . . allows a space for distinguished thinkers to write about their passions.'
The Philosophers' Magazine

'. . . deserve high praise.'
Boyd Tonkin, The Independent (UK)

'This is clearly an important series. I look forward to receiving future volumes.'
Frank Kermode, author of Shakespeare's Language

'both rigorous and accessible'
Humanist News

'the series looks superb'
Quentin Skinner

'. . . an excellent and beautiful series.'
Ben Rogers, author of A.J. Ayer: A Life

'Routledge's *Thinking in Action* series is the theory junkie's answer to the eminently pocketable Penguin 60s series.'
Mute Magazine (UK)

'Routledge's new series, *Thinking in Action*, brings philosophers to our aid . . .'
The Evening Standard (UK)

'. . . a welcome series by Routledge'
Bulletin of Science, Technology and Society (Can)

'Routledge's innovative new *Thinking in Action* series takes the concept of philosophy a step further'
The Bookwatch

To Dan

Acknowledgements ix

Introduction 1

Defining and Describing Privacy 3
The Different Meanings of Privacy 5
Democracy 8
Freedom/Liberty and Equality 11
Rights: Moral and/or Legal 12

Privacy and Democracy   One   17

The Secret Ballot 24
Privacy and/or Democracy? 28

Privacy, Equality and Freedom of Expression   Two   31

Oliver Sipple and the Ethics of Outing 31
Privacy and the Ethics of Publication 34
Privacy, Freedom of Expression and the Press 40

Privacy: The Family, Sex and Reproduction   Three   47

An Englishman's Home Is His Castle 48
Privacy Beyond the Home 54
Privacy, Romance and Realism 62
Privacy, Rights and Duties 64
Personal and Collective Responsibility 66

Privacy, Property and Solidarity **Four** 71

Thomson's Critique of Privacy 71
Privacy and Collective Property 76
Privacy and Private Property 79

Conclusion 85

Notes 87
Index 97

Acknowledgements

Sarah Richmond, Matt Finkin, Jeffrey Reiman, Nicolas Vrousalis, Axel Gosseries and Jonathan Wolff, all read parts of this book in manuscript and used their expertise to improve it. Joshua Cohen and Melissa Williams have provided much-needed advice over the many years since I first started writing on privacy as a graduate student. I am very grateful to them all, as I am to my kind editors at Routledge, and particularly to Andrew Beck, who have been models of patience and understanding and a fount of good ideas. I would also like to thank John Harris and the members of the Institute of Science, Ethics and Innovation, the University of Manchester, for a fellowship that enabled me to write most of this book in a lively and supportive setting, and Philippe Van Parijs and the members of the Chaire Hoover at the Catholic University of Louvain, who invited me for a three month visit. An invitation to join the Political Science Department, at the University of Geneva came as I was finishing the last part of this book, and has made finishing it so much easier. In a book on privacy it is fitting, as well as a pleasure, publicly to thank my parents, siblings, partner and children for their support and forbearance.

Introduction

Privacy is a Janus-faced value. It enables us to shut the world out, but the forms it takes and the extent to which it is protected are fundamentally public matters. Not surprisingly, then, privacy and its protection are the object of considerable public interest and controversy concerning the proper role of the state, and the rights and duties of individuals.

This book explores the Janus-faced features of privacy, and looks at their implications for the control of personal information, for sexual and reproductive freedom, and for democratic politics. It asks what, if anything, is wrong with asking women to get licences in order to get pregnant and have children, given that pregnancy and childbirth can seriously damage your health. It considers whether employers should be able to monitor the friendships and financial affairs of employees, and whether we are entitled to know whenever someone rich, famous or powerful has cancer, or had had an adulterous affair. It considers whether we are entitled to privacy in public and, if so, what this might mean for the use of CCTV cameras, the treatment of the homeless and the provision of public facilities such as parks, libraries and lavatories.

Above all, the book seeks to understand whether and, if so, why privacy is valuable in a democratic society, and what implications privacy has for the ways we see and treat each other. The ideas about privacy we have inherited from the past are marked by beliefs about what is desirable, realistic and possible which predate democratic government and, in some cases, predate constitutional government as well. Hence, this book argues, although privacy is an important democratic value, we can only realise that value if we use democratic ideas about the freedom, equality, security and rights of individuals to guide our understanding of privacy.

This book is a political theorists' approach to privacy. It places privacy in the spotlight set by familiar ideas about politics and morality, the better to understand and assess the contradictory claims about its nature, content and importance which can be found in the ever-growing number of books and articles on the subject. Ranging from the highly abstract and speculative to the detailed analysis of particular laws and regulations, the ordinary reader (or philosopher) is likely to be bewildered by their variety, and the seeming impossibility of fitting them together into a coherent picture.

I cannot promise to provide this coherent picture, but I hope to supply a sufficient sketch of the subject that readers will be able to fill in that picture for themselves. I have tried to keep the scholarly apparatus of endnotes to a minimum, so references at the back of the book provide links to on-line information, and to books and articles that might interest non-specialists. My hope is that readers who are not academics will be able to enjoy the book without much difficulty, but that its ideas and method will be sufficiently novel to please those who already have some expertise on the subject.

Chapter 1 looks at the reasons why intelligent, well-meaning and thoughtful people disagree about the nature and value of privacy, and considers how the secret ballot—once condemned as inimical to political freedom, now a staple of democratic government—might help us to approach these disagreements.

Chapter 2 looks at the ethics of outing—or the publication without consent of true personal information—and shows that privacy protections for confidentiality, anonymity and seclusion can enhance, rather than undermine, freedom of expression and democratic politics. Chapter 3 looks at the implications of privacy for sex, reproduction and the family and shows why the right to live with, and to look after, those we love is central to a democratic perspective on privacy. Finally, Chapter 4 examines the relationship between privacy and property ownership, and its consequences for social cooperation.

However, first, we need some philosophical scene-setting. Dramatists start their plays with a little preface such as this: 'It is the 1950s. Annie, who is 5ft. 2 and sitting, knitting, by the window . . .' For philosophers, scene-setting principally consists in comments on terminology and working assumptions—but the general purpose is the same: to prepare the mind's eye for the action that follows, and to make it easier to understand the plot as it unfolds. I hope that the following remarks will serve both purposes.

DEFINING AND DESCRIBING PRIVACY

A great deal of philosophical and legal debate about privacy concerns the best way to define it. Indeed, the difficulty of defining a right to privacy has been described as a stumbling block to the statutory recognition and protection for a right to privacy in the United Kingdom.[1] This is surprising, because it is doubtful that privacy really is any harder to define than any other complex right or value. In fact, the main reason why it is hard to define privacy—the absence of a set of necessary and sufficient conditions which would enable us to identify privacy and to distinguish it from allied concepts—suggests that the fuzziness of our concepts of liberty, equality and rights may, themselves, explain why the boundaries of privacy are hard to fix.

For example, we lack a sufficiently clear concept of liberty to decide whether your claim to prevent me from reading your diary is really a claim to *privacy* rather than to *liberty*, or what, if anything, follows if your claim can be described as examples of them both. Similarly, uncertainty about what it means to treat people as equals makes it difficult to know whether Joyce Maynard was morally entitled to publish her account of life with the famously reclusive author, J. D. Salinger. Publication undermined Salinger's privacy, while enabling Maynard to describe aspects of her experience as a talented 18-year-old writer, pursued by a distinguished, and much older, novelist.[2] But does this show that publication was unfair to Salinger, or failed to treat him as Maynard's equal? If the boundaries of privacy are obscure, then, this is partly because we are unsure how best to think about people's claims to freedom of thought, association and expression, and what it means to treat people as equals.

In so far as privacy is difficult to define, then, this is because our ideas about allied values, such as liberty and equality, are less clear than we sometimes think. No definition of privacy will remove that problem. Still, we will need to get behind the word 'privacy', and give it more shape and definition if we are to make progress in thinking about it. So, for the purposes of this book, I suggest that we think of privacy as referring to some combination of seclusion and solitude, anonymity and confidentiality, intimacy and domesticity. Whatever else the word 'privacy' is used to describe, it is used to describe these three groups of words; and whatever else talk of privacy as a moral or political right is meant to illuminate, it is normally meant to illuminate our rights and duties in these. Hence, thinking of privacy as some combination of these different things should help us to understand *what* people are arguing about when they argue about the value of privacy, and to understand *why* they may be unable to resolve their disagreements by pointing to facts about the world or the established meaning of words.

THE DIFFERENT MEANINGS OF PRIVACY

Privacy is associated with a variety of rather different things, typically polarised around control of personal space, personal information, and personal relationships, because privacy sets limits to the way that outsiders can interfere in our lives. Thus, some synonyms for privacy refer to seclusion, to selective access to an area such as a garden, or a house or apartment, and also to its exclusive or selective, rather than inclusive, character. When associated with control of information, synonyms for privacy centre on ideas of confidentiality, anonymity, secrecy, limited disclosure and control of access to information—whether factual, artistic, scientific, legal, religious or metaphysical. Finally, when referring to relationships, privacy is associated with the intimate, the sexual, the familial and the domestic.

These are rather different things, and though it is fairly easy to see certain practical, historical and psychological associations amongst them, the things 'privacy' refers to are not tightly related from a logical or a normative perspective. For example, private space can foster the ability to tell people we know and trust things that we would not want to share with other people, and to share jokes, confidences and practical information in ways that enhance our ability to define and shape our relationships. But it can also prevent us from discovering who knows what about us, who has been saying what about us, and who plans to do what to us. So, privacy can foster hypocrisy, deceit and mistrust rather than frankness, mutual confidence or love.

Nor is that all. Within each category, the things to which privacy refers seem only loosely connected to each other, which makes it hard to tell whether there is any logical or conceptual connection between the different elements of privacy, as commonly understood, or if they are just connected by happenstance, custom and convention. For example, exclusivity can foster seclusion, whether we are thinking of exclusive clubs and dining societies, gated housing associations for the rich, or very up-market jewellery and clothing stores, with their sentries on the door and deliberately intimidating personnel. Still, if seclusion is an attribute of exclusivity, exclusive use, access and ownership are not intrinsic to seclusion. In fact, how necessary they are probably depends on our access to public spaces like parks, gardens, roads and countryside, as well as to cinemas, museums and other public buildings which can be quite deserted and peaceful, although they are supposed to be open to all-comers.

So the different aspects of privacy, as used to refer to control of information, are not intimately connected. Nor can anyone who has much experience of the sexual, the domestic or the familial suppose that these all refer to the same thing, even if the one often leads to, and is associated with, the other. Indeed, many aspects of our supposedly intimate relationships are so bound up with complex social conventions and legal requirements that they may say less about us and our desires, interests, needs and feelings than about the society we live in, or the needs and desires of others.

It is scarcely surprising, then, that some people agree with the moral philosopher, Judith Thomson, that talk of 'a right to privacy' is so confused and confusing, referring to so many seemingly unrelated things, that it would be best, instead, to refer to people's rights over their property and over their person.[3] Nor is it surprising that the many philosophers and legal scholars who think Thomson quite mistaken nonetheless disagree about which aspects of privacy really are central to understand it as a value, or as a right.[4]

In due course, we will want to look at some of the controversy surrounding Thomson's claim that privacy is a confused and confusing way of talking about things that matter. The point of bringing it up now is not to try to resolve such debate at the outset, in so far as it is resolvable, but to explain why we should avoid committing ourselves to any particular definition of privacy at this point.

As we have seen, the term 'privacy' seems to refer to a cluster of heterogeneous things. It is also clear that the term can be used with linguistic propriety and effectiveness in all these different ways. So, while it would be wrong to assume that this one word really refers to one concept, rather than to a cluster of somewhat contradictory ideas, it also seems wrong to assume that what we've got is an unintelligible mish-mash that needs to be replaced entirely, or that can only be rendered coherent by radical surgery. Thus, with apologies to those who prefer philosophical investigations to be prefaced by myriad definitions, this book will not advocate or defend a particular definition of privacy, on the grounds that this task—if necessary or useful—may be easiest to accomplish once we have a better sense of the philosophical terrain involved.

Still, we are not going to get far in understanding privacy without trying to clarify our assumptions about liberty, equality, rights and democracy. As will be evident by now, none of these terms is self-explanatory and all are likely to be the object of considerable conceptual and normative disagreement.

My suggestion for dealing with this disagreement is to try to stick to fairly agreed and uncontroversial understandings of each of these terms and, where this is not possible, to explain and justify my particular assumptions about what it is to treat people as free and equal, or what it is to protect, rather than undermine, people's rights. What we need is enough clarity to understand disputes over the relationship of privacy to liberty, equality, security and solidarity without engaging all the exciting, complex, frustrating and, perhaps, irresolvable disputes which preoccupy specialists. So, before wrapping up this introduction, I will say something briefly about the way I will be approaching the terms democracy, liberty, equality and rights—as these are essential tools for our investigation of privacy.

DEMOCRACY

Just as privacy has many meanings, whose merits are controversial, so with most of the other concepts with which we will be concerned in this book. Democracy, for example, has been used to describe the government of Athens, when it was a slave-owning city-state which excluded women from citizenship. Alexis de Tocqueville used the word to describe modern societies that had broken down feudal social distinctions—between nobles, free-men and serfs, for example—and were increasingly breaking down distinctions of sex, race and class, even if, as in nineteenth-century Britain, they still lacked universal suffrage or 'one person, one vote'.⁵ However, I will follow standard contemporary usage in referring to democracies as countries whose governments are elected by universal suffrage and where people have an equally weighted vote.

I will also assume that democracies require 'one rule for rich and poor' and for governors and governed—that they are constitutional governments—although the extent to which democracies must have formal systems of law, and distinctive legal institutions, is by no means settled. Still, whether democracies have the clear separation of powers that Americans aim for, and whether or not they make room for customary law of various sorts, I assume that democracies must have well-known and generally effective protections for political, civil and personal freedoms of association, expression and choice.

Democracies on this picture can take many forms—some will look more like Brazil or India, others more like Sweden, Switzerland, Italy or America. However, allowing for the familiar gaps between ideals and reality, they will all entitle people to form a variety of associations through which to advance their interests, express their ideas and beliefs, and fulfil their duties as they see them. Democracies, therefore, are characterised by protection not just for political parties, unions, interest groups and churches but also by the protections they secure for soccer clubs, scientific societies, families, charities, and associations of the like-minded.

As we will see, controversy over privacy importantly turns on the implications of protecting privacy for family life, the regulation of the economy and the security of the state. So we will be unable adequately to understand the nature and justification of that conflict, or the extent to which it might be resolvable, unless we recognise the variety of forms of association, expression, identification and choice which characterise modern democracies.

Later, we will need to think a bit more about which political, civil and personal liberties we think people should have, in order to decide whether or not the consequences of valuing privacy are acceptable, unacceptable or positively desirable. At that point, I will suggest that we refine our picture of democracy, using familiar assumptions about the distinctive features of democratic government, and familiar assumptions about the different liberties, opportunities and rights that democracies require, permit or might come to espouse.

For example, I will suggest that we use the secret ballot—or the freedom to cast our votes in private—as an example of a democratic liberty, both because it is now almost as uncontroversial a feature of democratic government as universal suffrage itself, and because it reflects two ideas critical to contemporary democratic theory and practice. The first is that citizens with no special virtues, knowledge or resources are entitled to an equal share in government. The second is that democracy is a competitive as well as a cooperative business. While we all share interests in being governed democratically —at least, as compared to the most likely alternatives—we may have rather different ideas about which of the competing candidates for political office deserve our allegiance or support, and may stand to gain or lose a good deal depending on which party or set of individuals comes to power as a result of a democratic election. So, using this familiar and pretty uncontroversial example of a democratic right, and familiar assumptions about democratic government, should make it easier to investigate the value of privacy, and the controversy surrounding it.

FREEDOM/LIBERTY AND EQUALITY

Clarifying the way I will be using the word democracy helps to explain the meaning I ascribe to words like 'freedom' and 'equality'. Completely different things have been taken to epitomise freedom and equality. Thus, Aristotle thought that slavery was consistent with equality, because he assumed that there were natural slaves and natural masters.[6] Some people, like Robert Nozick, have wanted to define freedom in such a way that people could freely engage themselves to be the slaves of others. Nozick's understanding of freedom, in other words, included being a slave, on condition that one had voluntarily given up one's freedom under suitable conditions.[7] This claim strikes many people as unreasonable, because slavery seems like the antithesis of freedom, not an instance of it. Those of us who think that way will, therefore, need to find some other way of understanding freedom.

The trouble is that rejecting Aristotle's account of equality and Nozick's account of freedom still leaves us with myriad plausible, but mutually inconsistent, ways of thinking about what it is to be free, and whether or why freedom matters. If we are to make progress in understanding *privacy*, however, we are going to have to make some simplifying assumptions here, too. The ones I suggest that we make are these: that we take whatever forms of liberty are uncontroversially necessary to democratic government as examples of freedom; and we take whatever forms of equality are uncontroversially necessary to democratic government as examples of equality.

We will, in due course, have to decide what these are—but, for now, I think we can assume that if the right to choose your government and the right to stand as a member of that government are examples of democratic freedoms, they are also examples of democratic equality, because these are freedoms to which people are equally entitled, or which belong as much to the poor and the newly-naturalised citizen as they do to the rich and to those with a revered national pedigree. So, taking some familiar features of democratic government can help us to clarify our ideas about freedom and equality, and can give us a shared reference point for resolving disputes about the relationship of privacy, liberty and equality.

RIGHTS: MORAL AND/OR LEGAL

We are now in a position to clarify the last of our critical terms, 'rights'. The word is ambiguous, because it does not tell us whether we are concerned with legal rights or moral rights. Legal rights, unsurprisingly, are those rights which are recognised and protected by law. This is more complex than it first seems because not all rights on the statute books are enforced or will ever be enforced—some of them are there simply because it would be too much trouble to take them off the books. Nor are all legal rights statutory rights—some are constitutional and, in common law countries, such as Britain, some rights are declared by judges, reflecting on legal traditions as evidenced by custom and past judicial decisions and writings. So, what actually counts as a legal right can be a tricky business—which is why being a lawyer is a relatively well-paid profession!

However, what we need to remember is that the term 'rights' is ambiguous, because not all talk of rights refers to legal rights. Instead, some of our claims about rights refer to what we might call our 'moral rights', the rights to which we are entitled, whether or not the law actually respects and protects those entitlements. Sometimes we want to talk about moral rights to indicate what we think the law should be—or to highlight the fact that we think existing laws or governments are wrong or unjust. Thus, we may insist that people have a right to freedom of religion, even though the country that they are in recognises no such legal right and has just imprisoned a bunch of people for practising their religion. At other times, we are simply expressing the belief that people are morally entitled to something—to be treated kindly, to have promises kept and so on—either leaving it open what the law should do about this, or assuming that the situation we are concerned with is not a legal matter at all.

The relationship of moral and legal rights, then, can be quite complicated, because the former are sometimes used as the grounds for an argument or critique of the latter. Though intuitively we might suppose that you need to establish that something is a moral right in order to show that it is a legal right, a moment's thought about speed limits and tax laws makes it clear that this is mistaken. Moral rights may set the range within which considerations of convenience, efficacy, noise abatement, pollution, and so on determine the choice of speed limit in town and on the highway. Likewise, moral rights may set the range within which governments are entitled to choose which taxes to raise, how to raise them and at what rate to set them. Nonetheless, it would be a mistake to suppose that the reason why UK highway laws are justified (in so far as they are justified) is because people have a moral right to drive at thirty, rather than forty, miles an hour in town, and at seventy, rather than eighty, miles an hour on highways. On the contrary, in so far as people are morally entitled to drive at these speeds in the UK, it is because this is the legally accepted speed, recognised by law, and by the ways in which people generally behave when they are driving in the UK.

In short, one of the difficulties about the term 'rights' is that it can refer to both moral and legal rights, although these can be quite different things, with a rather indeterminate relationship to each other. I will, therefore, try to use the expressions 'moral right' and 'legal right' where necessary to avoid ambiguity. However, I will be supposing that talk of moral rights is a permissible and useful way to talk about what people are morally entitled to; and I will be assuming that at least some laws are justified. So, I assume that Bentham was wrong to think that talk of moral rights is 'nonsense upon stilts',[8] even though some claims about moral rights are nonsensical or absurd; and will assume that those anarchists who think all laws are unjust are wrong, even though many laws are, unquestionably, unjust. I doubt that these assumptions will be particularly controversial for people who are interested in the nature and value of privacy—both because utilitarians can, if they wish, parse talk of moral rights as claims about what utility permits or requires; and because anarchists who are interested in privacy will be interested in many of the questions about the relationship amongst individuals, that will concern us here.

As with freedom and equality, so with rights, we can use standard democratic rights to illustrate people's legal and moral rights, bearing in mind that the precise relationship of the legal and moral is a matter of controversy in most democracies. So, we can think of the right to vote as both a moral and a legal right—a right which, in democratic countries, is legally protected partly because people are morally entitled to participate in forming their government. We can, therefore, ask—as we will soon ask—what conclusions, if any, we can draw about people's moral claims to privacy from the fact that democracies grant citizens a legal right to vote secretly rather than openly? At all events, problems clarifying the idea of a right can be resolved in the first instance by thinking about familiar democratic rights—whether legal or moral.

That, I hope, is enough clarification to be going on with, and it is now time to turn to the problem of what value, if any, privacy might have for a democratic society.

Privacy and Democracy
One

There are at least two ways to think about the value of anything, including privacy. The first is to treat it as instrumental to something else, which one knows or assumes is valuable; and the second is to treat it as intrinsically valuable, or valuable for what it is, rather than what it does. Conversely, we can think that something is bad because its consequences are bad in some way, or because we think it is bad even if, as sometimes happens, it is a bad thing which occasionally yields good consequences. We may feel that way about lying or cheating. On the other hand, we might believe that a charitable disposition is intrinsically good or praiseworthy even though its consequences are not always beneficial.

This four-fold division captures the main ways for thinking about privacy and there is something to be said for each of them. For example, philosophers like Stanley Benn and Jeffrey Reiman associate our willingness to grant other people privacy with respect for them, and see this as the heart of a non-consequentialist account of privacy's value.[1] What is morally wrong with staring at the victims of accidents on the motorway, they imply, is not that this brings motorway traffic to a crawl, or causes needless traffic jams, but that such behaviour inappropriately treats people who may be frightened, injured, even dying, as objects of idle curiosity, speculation and exclamation by those driving by. The appeal of such views is that it seems to explain why privacy can be valuable even though the consequences of wrongful invasions of privacy differ widely, because people differ in their tendency to be upset by the tactless or intrusive behaviour of others, and differ in the degree to which they are willing to expose their lives, bodies and possessions to others.

By contrast, James Rachels thinks that the value of privacy largely comes from the way it enables us to distinguish friends from colleagues and lovers from doctors.[2] Assuming that the ability to make such distinctions is desirable, he argues that privacy is valuable because it enables us to disclose and withhold information about ourselves in different ways and to different degrees, thereby enabling us to be business-like and professional with some people, and loving and nurturing with others. The implication of Rachels' account of privacy—like that, more recently, of Thomas Nagel—is that if privacy did not enable us to distinguish what we do and say in different situations, there would be no particular reason to value it.[3] Nor would there be any reason to think privacy valuable, on their view, if we conclude that the desire to be or say different things in different situations was undesirable—evidence of deceit, hypocrisy, fear or inauthenticity, say—rather than evidence of social sensitivity, respect and tact. So, one of the nice things about this account of privacy is that it seems to capture a common belief that if privacy is valuable, it is because it does something good, although the desire for privacy is sometimes morally discreditable.

However, there are difficulties in constructing instrumental and intrinsic arguments about value, and these difficulties are reflected in current debates on privacy. The main difficulty with instrumental arguments about privacy, is that even if privacy has beneficial consequences, this may not be a reason to value *privacy*, rather than its *consequences*. There may be other ways of achieving those beneficial consequences and these may have more attractive features or fewer defects than privacy. Or, it may be hard to determine how often, or how reliably, privacy produces these good consequences, in part because it is hard to determine the precise boundaries or characteristics of privacy. Very often, we also lack the empirical evidence necessary persuasively to resolve questions of cause and effect. So, the characteristic difficulty with instrumental arguments is that we can value the consequences that something produces without being sure that this is a reason to value the way it was produced.

Thomas Nagel's interesting account of the political importance of privacy faces these difficulties. Nagel believes that the breakdown of established conventions of privacy, since the 1960s, has led to two undesirable results. On the one hand, he thinks, political analysis and debate has been displaced by political gossip about the loves, personal habits and foibles of politicians and public officials while, on the other hand, greater understanding of the complexity and ambivalence of people's sexual lives and desires has been impeded by the rather infantile level of public discussion of sex.[4] On this view, privacy is valuable mainly for the good consequences to which it gives rise: the ability to focus on things that matter, rather than being overwhelmed or distracted by trivia, or seduced by reductive and simplistic ideas about people's character, based on sensational or prurient claims about their sexuality.

However, the factors shaping contemporary political debate and analysis may have less to do with changing norms of privacy, or any overall 'loss' of privacy since the 1960s, than with changes in the ownership, economics and regulation of the media, which have made it increasingly difficult to keep newspapers afloat financially, and have forced even 'highbrow' television and radio channels to compete for audience share and advertising revenue with more popular stations. Were this so, there would be no particular reason to expect respect for privacy to affect the quality of political debate—whether for good or ill. Indeed, in the UK, where people are more tolerant of homosexuality than they once were, and increasingly hostile to press efforts to expose the homosexual experiences or relationships of politicians, the appetite for serious political analysis seems no greater than it was twenty years ago, when people were far more censorious about homosexuality. So, Nagel's claims about the value of privacy depend on a causal link between privacy and the quality of public debate which, while suggestive, is hard to substantiate.[5]

However, claims that privacy is intrinsically valuable have their own characteristic problems. The familiar problem, which most of us will have encountered at some point, is the difficulty of persuading others that something is valuable when they do not find it valuable at all. The less familiar, but no less difficult, problem is that if we have conflicting pictures of value in mind, what I describe as intrinsically valuable may appear an example of instrumental value to you. People can distinguish one value from another in a variety of different ways, thereby affecting what counts as an example of intrinsic, rather than instrumental, value. Those who believe that privacy is intrinsically valuable, therefore, face a familiar set of difficulties in substantiating their arguments, although these difficulties may have less to do with the nature of privacy, per se, than with the difficulty of substantiating claims about intrinsic value.

For example, Jeffrey Reiman wants to show us that privacy is intrinsically valuable, rather than desirable because it produces *other things* which are valuable. But getting this argument to work requires us to agree *both* that the things which Reiman thinks are valuable are, indeed, valuable, and that they examples of *privacy*, rather than of something else. 'Privacy is a social practice', he explains.

> It involves a complex of behaviours that stretches from refraining from asking questions about what is none of one's business to refraining from looking into open windows one passes on the street, from refraining from entering a closed door without knocking to refraining from knocking down a locked door without a warrant. . . . Privacy is an essential part of the complex social practice by means of which the social group recognizes—and communicates to the individual—that his existence is his own.

So, Reiman's way of dealing with the difficulty of showing that privacy is intrinsically valuable is to identify something which he assumes we will readily agree to be valuable—our ability to see ourselves as moral persons or agents—and then to describe privacy as one of the elements, or constituent parts, of this valuable thing.[6]

This is a subtle and appealing account of privacy, and helps to explain why we can value privacy even if we have nothing to hide—when we're not preoccupied with keeping secret some nefarious or shameful past, some mortifying experience or embarrassing beliefs or conduct. However, the special importance of *privacy* to the process by which human infants are turned into moral agents is not wholly clear, because most of our rights convey, to some degree, the idea that there are certain things which people may not do to us, even for our own good. So, it is hard to know whether it is *privacy*, rather than freedom of expression, or John Stuart Mill's freedom of tastes and pursuits,[7] which makes it apparent that our bodies, minds and tastes are our own. Hence, even if we grant Reiman's assumption that it is desirable for people self-consciously to see themselves as moral agents, rather than to do as they ought unself-consciously, we may wonder whether he has adequately described and explained the reasons to value privacy.

It can be remarkably difficult to show that privacy is valuable, then, whether we try to explicate that value in terms of the good consequences which we associate with privacy, or with a value that we identify with its peculiar features, or properties. However, critics of privacy face comparable problems in substantiating their arguments. Thus, in a famous article, Catharine MacKinnon claimed that

> It is probably not coincidence that the very things feminism regards as central to the subjection of women —the very place, the body; the very relations, heterosexual; the very activities, intercourse and reproduction; and the very feelings, intimate—form the core of what is covered by privacy doctrine. From this perspective, the legal concept of privacy can and has shielded the place of battery, marital rape and women's exploited labor; has preserved the central institutions whereby women are *deprived* of identity, autonomy, control and self-definition; and has protected the primary activity through which male supremacy is expressed and enforced.[8]

But while MacKinnon is right that legal protections of privacy have often had these effects, it is less clear that this makes privacy inherently, and irremediably, sexist, as she implies. On the contrary, many feminists have been moved by Virginia Woolf's claim, in *A Room of One's Own*, that women's lack of privacy has been a major obstacle to their self-development and self-expression and a potent sign of their second-class status.[9] So, one could think that MacKinnon is largely right about the way that established philosophical and legal views of privacy have disadvantaged women compared to men—in part, by denying them privacy within their marital and sexual relationships—without supposing that this is unalterable or an inescapable feature of claims to privacy.[10]

We therefore seem to be faced with the question whether it is possible to draw any conclusions about the value of privacy, or will we just find that any claims we make about its value—however tentative and provisional—are doomed to failure? The answer to the first question, I think, is 'yes', and to the second question, is 'no'. Specifically, I will suggest that we can construct a democratic perspective on privacy out of fairly familiar ideas about what makes governments democratic rather than undemocratic, and some widely shared assumptions about the reasons to favour the former over the latter. This will give us some much needed points of agreement with which to examine competing claims about the nature and value of privacy, and can help us to see which disagreements about privacy we might be able to resolve, and what types of information, reflection or action we would need to resolve them.

So, let's start by looking at the different reasons to value privacy implicit in democratic protections for secrecy in voting. Although the secret ballot was once deeply controversial, it is now generally assumed to be an essential feature of democratic government—in fact, as essential as the right to vote itself. Reflecting on why people ought to be entitled to seclusion, anonymity and secrecy when voting, rather than having to 'stand up and be counted', can therefore help us to understand why privacy might be valuable, and what that value has to do with democratic ideas about freedom, equality and happiness.[11]

THE SECRET BALLOT

The standard justification for the secret ballot is that it is necessary in order to prevent corruption and coercion from undermining the fairness of elections. The secret ballot enables people who want to discuss their vote to do so—they are free to tell anyone they want how they voted, and to urge others to vote likewise. Hence the secret ballot is compatible with freedom of expression, including the freedom to ask other people how they intend to vote, or how they have voted. However, the secret ballot means that people are free to refuse to answer such questions, and cannot be legally required to do so. Prior to its introduction, voters were often faced with efforts to bribe, coerce or intimidate them into voting one way rather than another. The secret ballot does not wholly preclude such efforts, but makes them much less likely to succeed and, therefore, much less likely to occur. So, the standard justification for the secret ballot reflects the important point that there is an instrumental justification for the secret ballot, one which has nothing much to do with the value of privacy per se, and everything to do with the importance of preventing bribery and intimidation from wrecking democratic elections.

Still, the obvious advantages of the secret ballot in combating bribery and intimidation should not blind us to the difficulties of treating the secret ballot as justified only for this reason. Were the secret ballot justified only because it protects us from bribery and intimidation, we would have to suppose that, in their absence, there would be nothing wrong with forcing people to discuss their voting intentions and acts with anyone who asks. In fact, it was precisely because he believed this that, after much agonising, Mill voted against the secret ballot, on the grounds that by the 1860s voters should have no serious fear of bribery or intimidation, and could be expected to stand up to pressure from others.[12] More recently, Geoffrey Brennan and Philip Pettit have argued that the secret ballot is undesirable, although sometimes necessary.[13] So, if the standard justification for the secret ballot is correct, we would have to concede, with Mill, Brennan and Pettit, that there would be no objection to getting rid of it were it not that we were worried for the safety of voters and the fairness of elections.

This seems unlikely. Arguments for open voting suppose that because we can harm others by our vote, and vote on mistaken or immoral considerations, we should be forced to vote openly. That way, others can correct our mistakes and the prospect of being exposed as selfish, insensitive or stupid will promote morally sensitive and considered voting. However, open voting will only improve the quality of voting if there are enough other people willing and able to correct, rather than to ignore or approve, our defects. And, of course, we must assume that people who are immune to information and arguments when they are free not to listen to them will prove willing and able to accept them when forced to do so. So the case for open voting is problematic even if we abstract from problems of coercion and intimidation.

But the most serious problems with open voting lie elsewhere, and highlight the importance of privacy to democratic citizenship. Democratic citizens are *entitled* to vote whether or not others approve of this, or of their likely voting patterns. They are entitled to a say in the way that they are governed whether they are rich or poor, well educated or not. By contrast, no one has a right to represent others politically unless they have been selected for the task. While democratic legislators may be more vulnerable to intimidation than citizens—as they are relatively few in number, and hold special power and authority *qua* legislators—it is the former, not the latter, who must vote openly, not secretly. Legislators have duties of accountability that citizens lack. That is why the former have a duty to vote openly, although citizens, like legislators, can vote wrongly whether through fear, greed, carelessness, confusion or ignorance.

Secret voting for citizens, then, reflects an important democratic idea: that citizens' rights to vote does not depend on the approval of others, or on the demonstration of special virtues, attributes or possessions. While democratic rights to freedom of expression and association mean that citizens are free to consult anyone they want, the secret ballot means that they can share in collectively binding decisions without having to bare their souls to anyone who asks.

This is the core reason why the secret ballot is justified, and is justified even if secrecy comes at some cost to the wisdom, transparency and morality of decisions. However, there is a second reason why the secret ballot is so important from a democratic perspective which, like the first, connects the value of privacy to membership in a democratic society.

Advocates of open voting assume that public shaming can be used to prevent and punish careless, selfish or ignorant voting. But while it is possible that open voting might, on balance, improve the quality of voting, both public shaming and the threat of public shaming are hard to justify for wrongful voting. The problem is this: that public shaming is likely to be out of proportion to the harm committed, and out of proportion to the punishments, if any, deemed appropriate in similar cases.

Public shaming is a blunt instrument, and likely to fall hardest on those who are unpopular, poor, shy and inarticulate, rather than on those who have committed the worst offences. Nor do its punishments usually bear any relationship to the concerns for fairness, rehabilitation and prevention that constrain legal forms of punishment. So, even if it were possible that open voting really would cure careless, prejudiced or ignorant voting, it would fall foul of concerns for fairness and equality. Hence, modern democracies tend to be wary of public shaming as a way to prevent or to punish immorality: for its weight is likely to fall in ways that are morally arbitrary and that make it harder for us to see and treat each other as equals. For example, the French prohibit the publication of photos of people in handcuffs or police custody unless they have been convicted, and even in the United States, where the 'perp walk' is still allowed, the practice is often criticised as stigmatising and prejudicial.[14]

If these arguments are right, the justification of the secret ballot is more complicated than it first seems, both because secret voting for citizens, as opposed to legislators, helps to distinguish their respective power and duties, and because it reflects democratic concerns for the equality, public standing and fair treatment of citizens. In a society with freedom of expression, we do not need to be forced into mini-tutorials in order to consider contrasting approaches to voting, and to our duties as citizens. Nor will we lack opportunities to discuss our doubts, raise our questions, or advocate our beliefs about politics. However, the secret ballot means that we are not forced to try to defend our view of the world to others who may be unable to understand or sympathise with it. Nor are we at risk of being turned into a public example for the edification, or merely the entertainment, of others.

PRIVACY AND/OR DEMOCRACY?

The example of the secret ballot shows us that privacy can be important to people's freedom and equality even though protection for privacy means that we cannot prevent or punish all thoughtless, selfish, ignorant or exploitative behaviour. It shows us that privacy can be particularly important if the shy, unpopular, eccentric and vulnerable are to be able to participate in events of national importance, even though it is hard to know how far, in its absence, most citizens of representative democracies would suffer from threats of coercion or corruption. Finally, we have seen that the secret ballot reflects, and publicly embodies, the belief that most citizens, most of the time, can be trusted to exercise their rights and duties without being subjected to enforced tutorials, or intrusive public scrutiny of their intentions, beliefs and interests.

But can we really value privacy *and* democratic government? Does not the example of the secret ballot provide a misleading, rather than helpful, guide to the value of privacy, suggesting that privacy is more important to democratic government than it really is? After all, even in the case of the secret ballot, it seems that privacy places fairly severe constraints on the information we can demand of others, and on our ability to publish true facts about them. Yet freedom of expression, and of the press, are, by common consent, essential ingredients of democratic government, enabling us to hold the powerful to account for their actions, to publicise our beliefs and opinions about the proper conduct of public affairs, and to inform and freely debate matters that shape our lives as a society, and as individuals. While much of the information we need to discuss such matters is likely to take the form of statistical generalisations, in which people's particular characteristics and peculiarities have no salience or relevance, social scientists and historians know that the detailed study of a particular case or individual can illuminate the precise working of causal mechanisms which statistical correlations alone will not reveal, and may provide a vivid sense of events or problems which we might otherwise dismiss as bland, boring or trite.

What, then, can we learn about the value of privacy by considering the constraints that it places on freedom of expression? Is privacy worthless whenever it makes it difficult or impossible to publish true facts about people? If the answer we give to that question is 'yes', it looks as though we will have to kiss privacy goodbye, and conclude that the secret ballot is no guide at all to the value of privacy. If, on the other hand, we decide that the answer is 'no'—that privacy can be valuable even if it sometimes conflicts with the discovery and dissemination of true information—what conclusions, if any, can we draw about the importance of privacy, and of the best way to protect it in democratic societies?

In order to answer these questions I suggest we start by exploring the ethics of 'outing'—or the publication, without consent, of true facts about a person's sexual orientation. We can then generalise the example to consider the publication, without consent, of true information about people's health or conduct more generally and, from there, try to draw some conclusions about the nature of people's interests in privacy, and their implications for freedom of expression and freedom of the press.

Privacy, Equality and Freedom of Expression
Two

OLIVER SIPPLE AND THE ETHICS OF OUTING

Oliver Sipple was a former US Marine, injured while serving in Vietnam. Sipple lived in San Francisco, and on 22 September 1975, he joined the crowd gathered outside the St Francis Hotel to see President Ford. He was standing beside Sara Jane Moore, when she pulled out a gun to shoot the president. Sipple managed to deflect her aim, and to prevent further shots. The police and the secret service immediately commended Sipple for his action at the scene. President Ford thanked him with a letter, and the news media portrayed Sipple as a hero.

Harvey Milk, San Francisco's openly gay City Councillor, and a friend of Sipple's, saw this as his chance to strike a blow for gay rights. So, without consulting Sipple, he leaked the fact that Sipple was gay to Herb Caen, of the *San Franciso Chronicle*. Caen duly published the news, which was picked up and broadcast round the world.

Though he was known to be gay among members of the gay community in San Francisco, and had even participated in Gay Pride events, Sipple's sexual orientation was a secret from his family, for whom it came as a shock. Outraged, Sipple sued the *Chronicle* for invasion of privacy, but the Superior Court in San Francisco dismissed the suit. Sipple continued his legal battle until May 1984, when a State Court of Appeals rejected his case on the grounds that Sipple had, indeed, become news, and that his sexuality was part of the story. Sipple died in February 1989, aged 47.

Sipple's story has several distinctive features. Most notably, Milk's intentions were not vindictive, and he clearly had no desire to hurt Sipple. His goal was to use Sipple's fame to remove the prejudice, contempt and fear of those who are sexually attracted to other members of their sex. So, by contrast with efforts to 'out' politicians who have lied about their sexuality, or who have condoned, even actively promoted, homophobia, Milk was not trying to threaten or harm Sipple. Indeed, Milk may not even have realised that Sipple would disapprove of his actions, or would suffer from the hostility of his family. Given his openly gay life in San Francisco, Milk may wrongly have assumed that there was no downside at all to outing his friend. Nonetheless, Sipple's case helps to illustrate the difficulties of outing as a political strategy, and points to the reasons why it is so often wrong to publish true facts about another person without their consent.

Several things seem to be wrong with outing Sipple. The first is that Milk's failure to ask Sipple for permission to talk to the press seems exploitative and contemptuous. After all, even if one's sexuality were altogether unremarkable, one might object to having it broadcast to all the world; and if it were likely to make one notorious, the subject of hateful abuse and, even, violence, one might well hesitate to have it widely known, even if one felt no shame about it. Hence, Milk's actions would be troubling even if we ignored the fact that, as Sipple's friend, he had duties to consider Sipple's interests and feelings that would not have applied to a stranger.

Second, Sipple's case highlights how easily we can be deceived (or can deceive ourselves) into thinking that we know more about other people's lives and interests than we do. Most cases of outing do not involve one friend outing another, but are motivated by anger at what is, or seems to be, the hypocrisy, injustice or selfishness of someone else. So Sipple's experience suggests that those doing the outing are very likely to underestimate the harm that that they inflict on others—both on their immediate victims, and on those who care for, or depend upon, them.[1] Hence, outing will often be unjustified on instrumental or consequentialist grounds— because its benefits are uncertain, unpredictable and, such as they are, may be achievable in other ways. By contrast, the harms are usually considerable, unavoidable and the full extent of the damage from outing can be easy to underestimate.

Outing means using someone simply as a means to one's own ends. Strikingly, the Sipple case suggests that this can be morally troubling even when those ends are ones which the victim shares, and has actively endorsed. And this interesting feature of the Sipple case points to the *political* dimension of *ethical* objections to outing, and to the ways that these differ from a consequentialist weighing of likely benefits and costs, or a Kantian concern with the ways that people can be misused by others. Those are objections to outing which we might have regardless of the society we live in, or our assumptions about the legitimacy of democratic government. By contrast, a political perspective on outing centres on the power which outing involves, and the difficulties of justifying this type of power from a democratic perspective.

Outing involves one person or a group claiming the right to make potentially life-changing decisions for a competent adult, although they have not been authorised to do so, are typically in no position to make amends for any harms they cause, and cannot be considered either impartial or expert judges of the claims which they propose to over-rule. This unilateral, unrepresentative and unaccountable power over others makes it difficult to reconcile outing with democratic politics. Hence, moral and political objections to absolute government, however benign or well-intentioned, help to explain what is ethically troubling about outing, even when it achieves legitimate objectives, including ones which have the support of its victim.

PRIVACY AND THE ETHICS OF PUBLICATION

Democratic concerns for freedom, equality and responsibility, then, mean that people ought to have broad, though not absolute, rights over true information about themselves, whether the point of publicising that information is to enlighten others, to entertain them, or to advance a legitimate moral or political cause. Publicising sensitive personal information, however true, undermines people's privacy, and threatens their social standing and equality with others. It turns some people into instruments for public amusement or edification regardless of the damage that this may do to their self-respect, their ability to command the respect, trust, affection and loyalty of others, and regardless of its impact on third parties.

Such publication, we are often told, is justified by the moral failings of the victim, whether those failings involve acts of hypocrisy, ingratitude, sexual infidelity, attention-seeking or, indeed, illegality.[2] But while our interests in controlling sensitive information may be self-serving, there is more to our interests in privacy than that. Control of personal information enables us to protect the feelings of other people, as Sipple's case shows, and to respond to their needs and concerns, even when we do not share them. Such control enables us to act with tact, discretion, respect, and out of a sense of duty, whether or not confidentiality protects our own interests. It enables us to distinguish what is owed to those who have cared for us, or for whom we have special duties of care, from what is owed to those for whom we have no special duties. In short our interests in confidentiality are not reducible to interests in avoiding embarrassment, pain, shame or indignity—important though these are—but include interests in meeting the needs and claims of others for whom, with all their limitations of imagination and sympathy, we may feel love, as well as duties of consideration and care.

Protection for privacy, therefore, can promote personal, as well as political freedom, and our ability to form a variety of personal, and political, ties to others. Whether our expressive interests are artistic, scientific, sexual or religious—and whether our medium of communication is gestures and behaviour or words and pictures—protection for privacy protects our ability to explore the world and our place within it, and to communicate what we have found to others without exaggerating its importance or having to vouch for its truth, beauty or utility. Thus, while it is natural for people whose lives revolve around the excitement and frustrations of scientific work to wish to talk about that with others who share those excitements and frustrations, it is equally natural that those whose interests are primarily familial—who want to discuss the new baby and its failure to sleep through the night—should be free to discuss that, without being obliged to bring the whole world into their discussion, or to pretend that their interest in discussing these matters is of significance to anyone but themselves.[3]

As Louis Brandeis recognised, your privacy interests in your diary do not depend on its economic or artistic value, or its importance for other people, but on the fact that you created its contents and do not wish to expose them.[4] Hence, he thought, you should be able to keep your diary to yourself, or to show it only to those you trust, even though your descriptions of beautiful sunsets, disappointments in love, hopes for the future are, when looked at objectively, entirely banal and unlikely to distinguish you from hundreds, perhaps thousands, of other people. Similarly, for your nightly chats with friends. These may be fairly generic, and unlikely to reveal anything damaging about you or them. But, even if you had nothing to fear were their content overheard, what is essential to many of our conversations is less the intrinsic interest of what we say, or the gestures we make, than their role in creating, recognising, cementing—or ending—our relationship with others.

Privacy enables us to give meaning to utterances and objects which, taken objectively, have no special value, just as it enables us to distinguish and give meaning to relationships and associations which reflect our different likes and dislikes, our different interests and, therefore, our particularity as people. Protection for privacy, then, enables us to express ourselves in ways that would otherwise be difficult or impossible because embarrassment, self-consciousness, shyness, the desire not to offend, the fear of boring others, or of exposing our ignorance prevent us from trying to articulate our thoughts, feelings and experiences, or from conveying them to others.

Some of that expression, of course, may be unattractive—selfish, boorish, racist—and the minds and bodies revealed may be feeble, lazy or ugly. And it is certainly true that some of the things that privacy enables us to say and do are—and ought to be—illegal, and therefore discoverable and punishable by law. But it is hard to see how people are to lead rich and satisfying lives if they are unable to differentiate their relationships with others; or how they are to fulfil their different duties unless they are able to identify, consider and order the different demands for attention, time and care to which these give rise. Hence, privacy protections for confidentiality and for intimate, as well as political, expression are important, enabling people to develop their moral and political capacities, including their sense of themselves as individuals, and as members of a potentially infinite number of different groups.

This is not to say that rights to privacy are absolute, or that they invariably trump rights to freedom of expression if, and when, the two conflict. These are not the implications of the secret ballot, which concerns true, but potentially sensitive, information about our political choices, identities, values and allegiances. So there is no reason to suppose it true when what is at stake is information about our personal choices, identities, values and allegiances.

If you are well known and obviously ill, you can expect to be the object of gossip and speculation. But it hardly follows that you should therefore have to anticipate what, now, is almost inevitable: the public broadcasting of such gossip, and its treatment as a means to fame and fortune by strangers. Likewise, if you are well known and seen to be staggering around drunk, or hanging out with people who are notorious, you can expect to be regarded unfavourably by those in the know. As John Stuart Mill emphasised, such knowledge and personal condemnation is the inevitable consequence of social life in a free society. As he puts it,

> A person who shows rashness, obstinacy, self-conceit—who cannot live within moderate means—who cannot

> restrain himself from hurtful indulgences... must expect to be lowered in the opinion of others, and to have a less share of their favorable sentiments.[5]

What is not inevitable, however, is the industrialisation of gossip and of its marketing to a mass audience as a form of entertainment, titillation and education.

Such industrialised gossip is hard to justify morally, even if we are inclined to think that it should be legal. As Stanley Benn argued, it is wrong to treat an entertainer's life simply as a source of entertainment,[6] because doing so wrongly treats the entertainer as a person with no feelings which can be hurt, and no aspirations or plans which can be harmed by our intrusive attention. Public education can usually be secured by means other than the unwelcome and enforced publicity which outing involves, just as it can usually be secured by means other than the compulsory public tutorials beloved by proponents of open voting. So, whatever legitimate purposes the publication of gossip serves can usually be met without humiliating and degrading people, however foolish or complicit they may have been in their humiliation.

Moreover, it is usually invidious publicly to single out particular individuals as a lesson for others—whether of the evils of abusing alcohol or drugs, the virtues of monogamy, the temptations and pitfalls of fame—when hundreds, perhaps thousands of other victims might have been chosen with equal justification and success to illustrate the lesson. This is especially true when the tutor is self-appointed, not demonstrably of good character, and often incapable of acknowledging, let alone of rectifying, the damage caused by the lesson. As in the case of outing by a single individual, such as Milk, so with the publication of salacious, embarrassing, amusing or surprising gossip by journalists: the justification for publicity, in any particular case, is likely to seem artificial, speculative and unpersuasive, and to beg the question of why *this* individual is entitled to over-rule the desire for privacy of *that* particular person.

Still, outing is not always immoral. Sometimes there is no other way to challenge damaging forms of hypocrisy, manipulation and prejudice than to expose those involved— or no way to do so that does not involve comparable harms to the interests and rights of others. Given the importance that the Conservative Party attached to 'family values' as a guide to economics and public morality when Margaret Thatcher was prime minister, it was scarcely surprising that ministers, such as Cecil Parkinson, who were engaged in adulterous affairs were 'outed' by journalists and, as in his case, forced to resign their ministerial position.[7] Nor does it seem unreasonable to ask Prime Minister Blair whether or not he had had his children vaccinated, given the furore around the safety of the MMR vaccine at the time, and his public assurances of its safety and importance to public health.[8]

By contrast, while illegal behaviour opens us to legal investigation, punishment and prosecution, we are not always justified in publicising such behaviour, or of reporting it in a way that is likely to make it the subject of wide attention, speculation and discussion. Laws are sometimes unjust and, even when justified, their violation may not be evidence of bad character or ill will, rather than of momentary distraction, or of depression, mental confusion, and despair. So, even in the case of illegal behaviour, what we are justified in publicising depends on our personal or professional responsibilities, and the alternatives before us, rather than on the legal status of the behaviour alone.

PRIVACY, FREEDOM OF EXPRESSION AND THE PRESS

People's claims to treat true facts about themselves as private, then, can be hard to evaluate. Immorality or illegality does not automatically deprive us of claims to privacy in true information about ourselves. Whether or not they do, it seems likely, depends on the importance of the particular rights to privacy for our freedom, equality and social standing, and of their relative importance compared to the moral and political considerations which would justify us in breaching that privacy.

For example, the gravity of election fraud, from a democratic perspective, would justify legal scrutiny of ballots by election officials, although duplicitous voting would not, even though the former might have been conducted with the best of intentions, and with no evident effect on electoral outcomes, whereas the latter may have meant breaking a legally binding promise, or committing a grave moral wrong. Similarly, the public importance of accurate information about whether Steve Jobs is seriously ill is different from the public importance of accurate information about the HIV status of a retired, albeit revered, sportsman like Arthur Ashe. Millions of people are unavoidably affected by the fate of Apple, and the legal obligations of a great many people will be affected by Jobs' health, given its likely implications for the financial status and prospects of Apple. So while it is easy to sympathise with Jobs' efforts to keep his ill-health secret, there are good reasons to think that he had moral obligations truthfully to disclose that he was suffering from cancer, so long as he intended to maintain his position at Apple.[9]

By contrast, the ill-health or imminent death of someone like Ashe might well be a source of sadness to people who had not known him personally, but who had admired his

PRIVACY, FREEDOM OF EXPRESSION AND THE PRESS

People's claims to treat true facts about themselves as private, then, can be hard to evaluate. Immorality or illegality does not automatically deprive us of claims to privacy in true information about ourselves. Whether or not they do, it seems likely, depends on the importance of the particular rights to privacy for our freedom, equality and social standing, and of their relative importance compared to the moral and political considerations which would justify us in breaching that privacy.

For example, the gravity of election fraud, from a democratic perspective, would justify legal scrutiny of ballots by election officials, although duplicitous voting would not, even though the former might have been conducted with the best of intentions, and with no evident effect on electoral outcomes, whereas the latter may have meant breaking a legally binding promise, or committing a grave moral wrong. Similarly, the public importance of accurate information about whether Steve Jobs is seriously ill is different from the public importance of accurate information about the HIV status of a retired, albeit revered, sportsman like Arthur Ashe. Millions of people are unavoidably affected by the fate of Apple, and the legal obligations of a great many people will be affected by Jobs' health, given its likely implications for the financial status and prospects of Apple. So while it is easy to sympathise with Jobs' efforts to keep his ill-health secret, there are good reasons to think that he had moral obligations truthfully to disclose that he was suffering from cancer, so long as he intended to maintain his position at Apple.[9]

By contrast, the ill-health or imminent death of someone like Ashe might well be a source of sadness to people who had not known him personally, but who had admired his gossip by journalists: the justification for publicity, in any particular case, is likely to seem artificial, speculative and unpersuasive, and to beg the question of why *this* individual is entitled to over-rule the desire for privacy of *that* particular person.

Still, outing is not always immoral. Sometimes there is no other way to challenge damaging forms of hypocrisy, manipulation and prejudice than to expose those involved—or no way to do so that does not involve comparable harms to the interests and rights of others. Given the importance that the Conservative Party attached to 'family values' as a guide to economics and public morality when Margaret Thatcher was prime minister, it was scarcely surprising that ministers, such as Cecil Parkinson, who were engaged in adulterous affairs were 'outed' by journalists and, as in his case, forced to resign their ministerial position.[7] Nor does it seem unreasonable to ask Prime Minister Blair whether or not he had had his children vaccinated, given the furore around the safety of the MMR vaccine at the time, and his public assurances of its safety and importance to public health.[8]

By contrast, while illegal behaviour opens us to legal investigation, punishment and prosecution, we are not always justified in publicising such behaviour, or of reporting it in a way that is likely to make it the subject of wide attention, speculation and discussion. Laws are sometimes unjust and, even when justified, their violation may not be evidence of bad character or ill will, rather than of momentary distraction, or of depression, mental confusion, and despair. So, even in the case of illegal behaviour, what we are justified in publicising depends on our personal or professional responsibilities, and the alternatives before us, rather than on the legal status of the behaviour alone.

achievements in the world of tennis, and his efforts to confront racial injustice and prejudice in the USA and abroad. Nonetheless, accurate information about Ashe's health had no obvious bearing on the moral or legal duties of strangers. Consequently, there was no reason why, during his lifetime, Ashe should have been threatened with the publication of his HIV status, or treated as a poster boy for the significance of non-homosexual transmission of the disease in the West.

It would therefore be wrong to confuse freedom of the press with freedom of expression, or to suppose that privacy and freedom of expression are antagonists, locked in a zero-sum game, in which gains to the one can only come at the expense of costs to the other. Our interests in being able to express ourselves freely, and to communicate with others, are varied and not reducible to interests in untrammelled access to other people's ideas and experiences. Hence, freedom of expression must be understood to include private jokes, codes, grumbles, complaints, expressions of love, hope, passion and need, or the ability to talk in ways that draw on shared experiences, meanings and ideas implicitly, rather than explicitly.

Protection for people's privacy, therefore, means that it should be legally possible to demand and win damages for wrongful invasions of privacy, and that the press should be regulated in a way that respects people's claims to privacy. Hence we cannot resolve conflicts over the respective claims of privacy and press freedom by assuming that the one is intrinsically more valuable than the other. Instead, we will have to identify and evaluate the expressive and privacy interests at stake, when conflict arises, bearing in mind that if the right to publish, in a democracy, does not depend on literary, moral or political merit, respect for privacy is not just for the virtuous, sensible or uninteresting. In some cases this means that autobiographical accounts of people's lives will have claims to invade the privacy of other people which will be lacking in journalistic and biographical accounts of seemingly similar subject-matter.

There is, for example, little to recommend the average 'kiss and tell' story, recounting the one-night stand, or lengthy affair of someone who is not famous with someone who is. The format does not lend itself to much variation or reflection, but provides an excellent vehicle for personal grudges, self-justification and self-congratulation. However, citizens must be free publicly to describe their lives and affairs, to use their lives as art, as science and as an example to others. Because our lives are bound up in the lives of others, it follows that if we are legally entitled to describe and publicise the details of our lives, there is much about the lives of others which we must be legally entitled to publish also, and which we must be able to publish without their permission. Otherwise, most people would find it nearly impossible freely to describe, discuss and publicly to explore the significant events, relationships, constraints and opportunities in their lives. This means that it must be legal to publish stories, autobiographies and reports which are of questionable quality and taste, and which exhibit moral failings such as selfishness, complacency, insincerity and dishonesty, so long as they are not libellous or defamatory.

'Kiss and tell' stories, therefore, are an example where the privacy interests of those who wish to avoid publication are unlikely to justify legal constraints on a person's ability to publish 'their story', and to profit financially from the legal freedom to do so.[10] However, this does not mean that protection for privacy has no role in determining other aspects of the publication of 'kiss and tell' stories. For example, it may be desirable to limit how intensely, and how frequently journalists are allowed to pursue and try to question third parties to such stories, such as children and spouses, even if this makes it more difficult to question the story's author and its main subject. In the UK, for example, the families of those caught up in a media frenzy suffer from packs of journalists and photographers following them around; endless ringing of their doorbells and of their phones; the inability to leave the house without being surrounded by a scrum of journalists—in short, behaviour which looks very much like harassment and which is likely to be frightening for children, and even for the adults involved. No one's right to self-expression justifies such behaviour, nor is there any 'right to publish' or to know what people are feeling or thinking which does so either.

It may be also desirable for newspapers to report the sums they offered, and subsequently paid, for their 'kiss and tell' stories; to inform their readers whether they were the ones who solicited the story, or merely agreed to publish it, and so on. Were this standard practice, readers would be better placed to judge how far newspapers are being used to carry out a grudge or feud, and how actively they are instigating stories which, under the guise of autobiography, publicly describe and evaluate the private life of well-known figures.

Reporting the fees that such stories command may increase their supply for a while, and the invasions of privacy that accompany them. But it is public knowledge that selling one's story of sex with the famous is a way to make money and, even, to launch a career. So there is no reason why newspapers should not disclose the sums involved, and the way that they are negotiated. This would promote public understanding of the economics of a lucrative branch of journalism, and would make it easier to understand the market price, if not the value, of privacy.

However, autobiographical justifications for publishing privacy-invasive material do not automatically apply to third-person publications, whether biographical or journalistic. Where celebrities do not wish to relinquish their privacy, and have taken steps to secure it—for example, by not going out publicly together, being discreet, and so on—it is hard to see why journalists should be entitled actively to pursue them, and to publish stories about their sex lives. Such stories may be entertaining, even informative, but curiosity about the sex lives of consenting adults cannot explain why people who are otherwise entitled to privacy should be deprived of it. Hence, the reasons why it should be legal to publish 'kiss and tell' stories, invasive though they are of people's privacy, do not apply to those cases where none of the people involved wish to relinquish their privacy.[11]

This is not because autobiography is more important, more expressive or more interesting than biography, nor that it is morally superior to write about oneself than about other people. Often the reverse is true. Any democratic conception of freedom of expression will provide significant protections for journalistic and biographical accounts of people's ideas, actions and experiences, and the importance of protecting such expression will very likely justify limits on the privacy of politicians and other people who hold positions of political power and influence.[12] However, when it comes to stories about the sex lives of celebrities, or would-be celebrities, I have argued, people have a stronger claim to publish stories about their own lives, even if this means publishing details about the lives of others, than they do to publish stories about people who, however fascinating, have neither the desire nor the obligation to relinquish their privacy.

* * *

In the last two chapters, I have argued that we have important personal and political interests in confidentiality, which are intimately related to democratic ideas about the way power should be distributed, used and justified in a society. On that view ordinary people, with their familiar moral failings and limited, though real, capacities for sensitivity, altruism and wisdom are entitled to govern themselves and, in so doing, to take responsibility for the lives of others. This suggests that they are not in need of constant hectoring or supervision in order to act well, although they are rightly accountable to appropriate public authorities for their exercise of public powers, their use of public resources and their respect for each others' rights. Hence, as we have seen, people's claims to confidentiality do not depend on the usefulness of that confidentiality to others, or on the moral, aesthetic or, even, political and economic worth of the things that they wish to do with it.

In the next chapter, we will move from an investigation of the informational aspects of privacy to its associations with the sexual, familial and domestic. We have seen that in a democracy our words and thoughts do not have to be especially revealing, expressive, dangerous or embarrassing in order for us to be entitled to keep them to ourselves, any more than we have to show that they are of special aesthetic, scientific, moral or political importance in order to justify their publication. As we will see, this means that people must have considerable latitude in the conduct of their sexual, familial and domestic relationships, even if their intrinsic merits are uncertain, as is their value to others.

Privacy: The Family, Sex and Reproduction
Three

We have seen that protections for privacy can reflect people's claims to freedom, although privacy inevitably constrains what we know about each other, what we can say about each other, and what we may do to each other. We have also seen that privacy can protect the equality and dignity of individuals by protecting them from arbitrary forms of hostility and punishment, as well as from unfair aspersions on their character, judgement and motivation. This gives us some reason to think that people should be entitled to a good deal of latitude in the conduct of their sexual, familial and domestic affairs, because these are all areas of life in which we are peculiarly tempted to question the wisdom, virtue and decency of others, and too readily to assume the beneficence, self-evidence and validity of those forms of behaviour with which we are familiar, or to which we subscribe.

However, critics of privacy have complained that treating the family as private perpetuates arbitrary inequalities within and between families and wrongly skews social policy and social institutions in favour of those who are already powerful, popular and well-placed to pursue their interests.[1] This suggests that we can only think of the family, sex and reproduction as private matters at the cost of democratic commitments to freedom, equality and social solidarity. But is that really the case, or is it possible to care about the way family life replicates unjust patterns of power and privilege while valuing privacy?

In order to answer these questions I suggest we start by looking at the feudal associations implicit in the old tag that 'An Englishman's home is his castle'. Doing so will help us recognise the importance of freedoms that we often take for granted, and whose centrality to democratic government we tend to overlook. But it will also help us to think about the differences between democratic and undemocratic forms of family life, and to see what these differences imply for the nature and value of privacy in the workplace, in the military and in politics, as well as in the home.

AN ENGLISHMAN'S HOME IS HIS CASTLE

It might seem odd to take Coke's claim that an Englishman's home is his castle as a guide to the value of privacy in a democratic society, because of its sexist, nationalist and feudal associations.[2] Moreover, Coke's phrase is sometimes thought to mean that people are entitled to do whatever they want at home, which makes it sound implausible as a guide to either political or personal morality. However, murder at home is still murder and even feudal lords owed duties of obedience to their superiors, so 'anything goes at home' cannot be a correct interpretation of the rights and liberties implicit in Coke's phrase. A more plausible reading of it would seem to be this: that Englishmen are morally (and should be legally) entitled to *refuse to admit* other people to their home without seeking special permission for doing so; that they are entitled *to invite* people into their home without seeking special permission for doing so; that they do not need special permission in order *to hire or fire* people to work in their homes, or to *dispose* of their personal possessions, to marry and have children, or to manifest their approval or disapproval of the marriages that their children wish to make.

This, I think, is a rough and ready summary of the complex ideas bound up with the idea that an Englishman's home is his castle, although legal uses of the phrase tend to stress the right to exclude others from one's home, rather than the right to invite and shelter friends and allies. But why would the liberty to refuse entry to your home, or to invite friends and family to enter it matter to someone, such as a feudal lord, who is capable of defending himself militarily? Why are these freedoms worth having?

The answer, presumably, is that recognition of one's *entitlements* in such matters is precious, whether or not one needs to use them, reflecting a desirable moral and political status to which certain distinctive rights, duties, powers and immunities are attached. Where these entitlements are recognised and accepted, one does not need to use force in order to decide who will or will not enter one's home, or share one's hospitality and the advantages which that confers. Where these entitlements are recognised, in other words, one's own sense of duty, right, convenience, pleasure, security and economy are sufficient to determine who is and is not a guest in one's house, the beneficiary of one's duties as a host, and of one's special affection and consideration beyond that. Privacy so understood, reflects a desirable status of trust, power and responsibility, and gives one the liberty and opportunity to form ties of affection, influence and convenience without consulting one's superiors.

The importance of being able to marry and to dispose of one's property without consulting a superior is, if anything, even more critical to one's ability to act autonomously—albeit within the constraints imposed by custom and law—than the ability to regulate entry into one's house. However militarily powerful you are, if your superiors can forbid you to marry, they will have deprived you of the ability to pass on your name and genes through legally recognised heirs and, in a feudal society, will have deprived you of an important resource—yourself and your offspring—with which to advance your interests and protect yourself against the threats posed by old age, illness and infirmity. Likewise, if you can only bequeath your personal property with your lord's permission, then everything you own is effectively his, and even the mightiest baron becomes, in effect, a servant or steward acting only as his master desires.

So, a brief look at the practical and symbolic significance of the liberties implicit in the idea that a man's home is his castle suggests that the ability to grant and refuse entry to your home and hospitality can be of great importance even if it does not entitle you to do whatever you want at home. The ability to deprive people of such things can constitute a form of punishment, a weapon of intimidation, and signal of one's power and authority. So, reflection on Coke's dictum throws into sharp relief how much the personal happiness, security and equality of modern constitutional democracies is bound up in liberties which most of us, most of the time, take so much for granted that we do not even register their existence.

Freedom means that we are not constantly struggling with threats of coercion, exploitation and injury to ourselves and loved ones. But it also means that we have the ability to make plans with and for them, plans which depend on our ability to project ourselves into the future—in imagination, at least. If objections to our politics, religion, to the way we dress and eat, or to our friendships and habits of lovemaking are sufficient to deprive us of their company, or to force us to alter our plans, life will be so unstable that none of us will venture anything of emotional or material consequence in sexual and familial matters. Likewise, if others could deprive us of our parents, children, siblings or spouses simply because they want to, we would be unlikely to find in them the forms of solidarity, recreation, satisfaction and fulfilment which we now seek in them.

Of course, this brief excursus also highlights the difficulties of using Coke's tag as a guide to the value of privacy. If, on the one hand, it captures ideas about the content and importance of privacy which might readily be generalised to a society where people must learn to see and treat each other as peers, it is equally apparent that there are aspects of the ideal which simply cannot be generalised in this way.

The reason is simple: the tag assumes that there is only one master in any castle, and that that master is the male head of household, entitled to rule over and determine the fate of his wife, children and servants.[3] We might—and certainly should—seek to extend the insights into the value of privacy to wives and children, as well as to bachelors and domestic workers, both male and female. Still, it looks as though we will have to modify and curtail the powers suggested by Coke's image of privacy, unless we want to commit ourselves to the unappealing idea that the family should look like a gathering of powerful lords, each with unqualified powers to dispose of their property and company, despite sharing a common house.

Such a picture does not seem very familial, nor is it likely to lead to any durable association. Families, after all, are typically made up of people who are not all legally competent adults; who are not all equally healthy or gainfully employed nor, therefore, equally capable of doing as they please. Moreover, they generally comprise people who have moral and legal duties for each other, as well as moral and legal rights against each other, which reflect their special relationship, and are not reducible to the rights and duties a stranger would have. In short, because the point of families, generally, is that they are ongoing associations of interdependent people, united by special ties of affection, history, need, interest and responsibility, we cannot simply generalise a picture of privacy appropriate to a hierarchical society and expect it adequately to address the needs of a democratic society. So, if we want to get a better sense of the value of privacy for democratic, rather than feudal or aristocratic societies, we will need to think more carefully about the protections for moral and political agency suggested by Coke's dictum.

We might start by recognising that if the point of privacy is to protect people from threats to their agency, bodily integrity and security, then all people are entitled to protection for their privacy even though some people—children, the mentally incompetent and so on—may need others to exercise these powers on their behalf. So, the idea of one person—a male head of household—having claims to privacy which cover those of another person, or substitute for them, is unacceptable.

Hence the importance of the UK's Guardianship Act of 1973, which was passed in response to the success of Joan Vickers' private member's bill of 1965, and finally gave women legal guardianship of their children.[4] Before the passage of the Act, women in England and Wales had to seek the consent of their husbands, even if they were estranged from them, in order to open a bank account for their children, to obtain a passport for them and even to obtain surgery for them. In short, the laws of guardianship in Britain, into the 1970s, reflected the legacy of monarchical assumptions about the importance of locating ultimate power in an individual, rather than a group, as well as the sexist assumption that the ultimate locus of authority in a family must be male, not female.

Moreover, if the purposes of privacy protections are to support our agency, bodily integrity and security, then the limits of privacy would seem to be set by those things which threaten or actually violate our agency, bodily integrity and security. So understood, the reasons for controversy about privacy become fairly clear: should suicide, for example, be understood as a threat to our bodily integrity which the state should prevent, or an example of our agency, which it should accept?[5] And what about sex and childbearing? These, after all, can threaten our bodily integrity, as well as our lives and health, even when we willingly engage in them, and are capable of giving informed consent to the threats that they pose. And what about concerns for equality between, as well as within families, or social solidarity, even morality? How are these to figure in our understanding of what privacy can and should protect and, therefore, of its value?

Answering these questions, I think, is easiest if we consider what the threats to our agency, bodily integrity and security are, to which privacy is meant to be a protection. In modern constitutional democracies, unlike feudal regimes, we do not generally need privacy in order to avoid the worst forms of violence, but to ensure that we are able to pursue our own ideas of what makes life worth living in the face of the different opinions, beliefs and tastes of other people. The home is a refuge, in other words, less from the violence and intimidation of other people—though it can still be valuable for that reason—than from the strains of having to get on with people one does not much like; having to collaborate and cooperate with people who can be difficult, unpleasant, unpredictable, or frustratingly incompetent. What makes the home and family life special for many people is the chance to relax and 'be oneself', and the sense of being amongst people who can be expected to care how one feels, how one's day has gone, and what one's future looks like—and for whom, in turn, one feels genuine concern and affection.

PRIVACY BEYOND THE HOME

So, we can start to see why protection for sexual, not just artistic or political, expression and experiment, is central to privacy. As Joshua Cohen notes, our intimate relations with others—including our sexual relations with them—provide

> an important setting in which we do something of fundamental importance in a decently lived life, namely, work out a sense of our identity. But this importance of sexual intimacy . . . is contingent in part on its being guided by the judgements, feelings and sensibilities of the parties to it.[6]

Privacy protection for sex is a way of recognising that we need to be able to give expression to feelings, desires and beliefs about how we should live, although other people may hold quite different views about such matters, and must be free to urge those views on us, and to live by them, themselves. Hence, while the state has a duty to prevent and punish threats to our agency, bodily integrity and security in sexual, as in other matters, the means which it may use in pursuit of these ends need to be sensitive to the connections between people's interests in sexual expression, and their interests in independent judgement and action.

For example, while pregnancy and childbirth can be expected to be painful and to involve some significant risks to life and health, it would be unacceptable for the state to require women to get a licence in order to give birth; or to forbid it for those for whom it might be especially risky. To do so might have beneficial consequences overall, and it might have negligible effect on the lives of some women. But for others, such laws would be devastating, denying them a significant means of expressing their love and faith or, indeed, their sense of vocation and purpose in life. So, while the state should try to ensure that childbearing, though risky, is not dangerous or traumatic, state regulation of pregnancy, childbirth and abortion needs to recognise that the risks and pains, hopes and triumphs of pregnancy and childbirth are not purely physical—intense and dominating as these often are—but inextricably bound up with the values we seek in life, and in our relationship to others.

That is not to say that we must sharply distinguish public and private things, relationships and people. In some ways, what can be said of families can be said of small businesses, too, which are often the repository of as many hopes and fears, time, attention and resources as families, and as much the locus of collective ideals and of close personal relationships, as families. This is particularly true of family-owned and -run small businesses, where the parents may spend the great part of their time, and where children, and their friends, will often work after school, at weekends and during vacations.

Or consider the workplace. Much employment in the USA is 'employment at will', which means that the employers' will is held to determine the nature and length of the work contract.[7] This means that workers can be fired for 'good reason, bad reason, and no reason at all'. Hence, protections for privacy, taken for granted by European workers, may lack any purchase in the American workplace. For example, employees can be discharged for failing truthfully to answer detailed questionnaires about their personal life and the number of siblings they have; they can be fired because employers do not like the charitable or voluntary work that they do in their spare time. They can be subject to medical and drug tests, and the scrutiny of their email, the contents of their desks, their phone calls. They can even be required to conduct their personal brokerage trade with their employer, rather than with other firms, so that their employer can track their personal trading patterns more easily![8]

This lack of privacy seems to be an expression of a deeply inegalitarian picture of the employer–employee relationship, sharing more in common with that between an absolute monarch and his or her subjects, than between people who see each other as equals. Hence, it is difficult to reconcile democratic government with an idea of the workplace as a privacy-free zone, or one in which employee privacy is a privilege, dependent on the whim of employers.[9]

Likewise, even in military affairs, we should expect to find some protections for personal relationships, beliefs and activities. Just as protection for privacy is critical to the differences between democratic and feudal families, so it is critical to the differences between democratic and feudal armies. Recognition that people are entitled to form intimate and familial relationships with others means that armies cannot simply pressgang the young or unmarried to provide labour or sexual services for them; and that armies cannot persecute or mistreat soldiers because they are gay or female.[10] It also means that armies need to provide some means for soldiers to remain in contact with their families, and to visit them, rather than being separated indefinitely, or for years of service in distant lands, as was once the case. In other words, people's claims to family and domestic life do not cease because they perform military service, though they are likely to be more attenuated in some cases than they would be in civilian employment.

If these points are right, people's claims to privacy extend beyond the doors of their home, and help to structure social and political life, not merely family life. This is partly because privacy for sexual, domestic and familial relations requires protection from employers, unions, church leaders, educational authorities, the military and the government, but also because it is people's individuality, sociability and agency which privacy protection seeks to secure, and these extend well beyond domestic, sexual and romantic settings. For some people, their company is their baby, and people can invest their hopes, money and energies in artistic or scientific endeavours, seeking through these the personal satisfaction, companionship and excitement which others seek in sex, love and romance. The claims to associative freedom, self-direction and seclusion to which these give rise are not identical to those in families, just as they are unlikely to be the same as each other. But if the point of privacy is to support people's freedom and equality, people's claims to privacy cannot be bound by a narrow model of family life, or by the assumption that familial and non-familial associations can and should be sharply distinguished.

The fact that there is no bright and unbridgeable public/private line also means that demands for public standards of safety, equality, freedom, fairness and accountability can determine the shape of the private realm and form islands of public regulation in areas that are conventionally thought of as private, such as the family. Hence, even within the realm of the private, to use a familiar metaphor, objects, relationships and activities will count as private to different degrees, merit different degrees of privacy protection and, in some cases, will not be private at all.

For example, the state was not invading people's privacy when it passed laws specifying that the guardianship of children should belong to mothers and fathers equally. In principle, the UK's Guardianship Act of 1973 might have left it up to parents to decide which one of them to designate as legal guardian, or whether they would both hold guardianship jointly. For practical purposes, the state could have required all families to choose a guardian or guardians, and it could have provided procedures for families to alter these arrangements. Instead the Guardianship Act specified that both parents were to count as guardians for legal purposes, unless one or both of them was proved unfit.

Of course, had the Act let parents decide this matter for themselves, it would formally have increased parents' scope for private decision-making—for making decisions concerning their family affairs by themselves, and according to their own best judgements. However, without the legal requirement to include mothers as joint guardians of children with fathers, it is quite likely that many women would have been excluded from guardianship, whether they liked it or not. Their financial dependence would have made it difficult to insist on joint guardianship, and the force of precedent and of custom would have meant that the demand for joint guardianship would have seemed in need of a special justification that the 'natural', 'practical', 'convenient' option of sole male guardian would have seemed to lack.

There are very good practical and symbolic reasons, then, why we should celebrate the fact that the Guardianship Act insisted on joint guardianship, as opposed to some other alternative to husbands as sole guardians of children. But the important point, for our purposes, is that the state was not invading the privacy of parents when it determined laws of guardianship. The state has duties to ensure the wellbeing of children, and to frame and uphold the legal rights and duties of parents. These properly limit the claims of parents as a group, and as individuals.

The familial, sexual and reproductive, then, is not private in all respects, even though some of our strongest claims to privacy, morally as well as legally, fall within these categories. This is particularly important because though young men are more likely to suffer injury and violence outside the home than within it, the reverse appears to be true of women and children. Likewise, for too many families, poverty, deprivation, insecurity and homelessness are a feature of family life—whatever other benefits it may bring in absolute terms, or as compared to the world they experience at school, at work, on the streets or in care. And for some people privacy and family life are inseparable from the overwhelming burden and anxiety generated by the need to care for chronically sick or disabled adults and children.

Attention to these problems suggests both that privacy is not an unalleviated good—and that sometimes it is not a good at all. But it also suggests that efforts to promote equality and solidarity have an important role in creating and promoting valuable forms of domestic and familial life. Just as constitutional democracy is a precondition for forms of privacy that enable most people, most of the time, to distinguish their homes from fortresses, so anti-poverty programmes, effective schemes of safe and attractive public housing, even robust anti-discrimination measures, limits on hours of work, and cheap and accessible forms of public transport, may all be necessary if privacy is to be valuable, and enjoyed by the many, not just the fortunate few.

We have seen, then, that the idea that 'a man's home is his castle' helps to illuminate the value of privacy, by drawing our attention to the significance of forms of liberty, equality and security which, as members of a democratic society, we may often overlook. However, we have also seen that there are some important differences between undemocratic and democratic views of the nature and value of the sexual, familial and domestic, whether we contrast democracies with feudal societies or with more recent, and less extreme, forms of hierarchy and inequality.

Democratic protections for self-discovery and self-expression, then, are not limited to words and ideas, but apply also to people's bodies, relationships and associations. How we define the precise contours of the personal and collective rights to which these protections give rise is difficult whether we are concerned with moral or with legal rights, because neither the intrinsic value of our associations, nor their utility to others, provide sufficient grounds for their regulation. The different values that individuals seek in, bring to, and discover in their personal relationships is a reason to grant them considerable latitude in their formation, conduct and dissolution. However, concern for the freedom, equality and security of ordinary people, not merely of a privileged or fortunate few, means that democratic states are *obliged* to regulate people's familial and marital relations, as well as their economic or political ones, and *permitted* to engage in forms of scrutiny and of preference-shaping that, otherwise, would be unjustified. So, while the precise contours of the public/private distinction are controversial, people's claims to freedom of choice, association and expression do not depend on the possession of special wisdom, virtue, wealth or connections—whether we look at their public or their private dimensions.

Before concluding this chapter, I want to address two different worries about the conception of privacy that I've sketched so far. The first, is that these arguments for privacy fail to differentiate sex, reproduction and family life from other things—confidentiality for one's political or religious views, say, or objections to the state commandeering spare bedrooms, furniture and clothing to help the needy. Perhaps it is true that privacy protection for sex, marriage and family helps to promote people's freedom, equality and security but, we may think, is there not *more* to privacy protection for sex, love and family than that?

The second worry is rather different. If the first expresses concern at my somewhat deflationary view of family privacy, the second doubts that sex, love and the family can really be private. Granted that some things may be private, this objection suggests, how can privacy cover things as critical to the state and the wellbeing of society as sexual behaviour, reproduction and family life? In a society where people are each other's peers, not their superiors and inferiors, why is not the conduct of sexual, reproductive and familial affairs a collective, rather than a personal, matter?

These strike me as two natural and important objections to the picture of privacy that I've presented, and I will try to address each separately, before showing why a democratic perspective on privacy must accommodate the pragmatists amongst us, as well as the romantics, and must accommodate people's sense of responsibility, not just their powers of choice.

PRIVACY, ROMANCE AND REALISM

The first objection points to what we might call the deflationary account of privacy for sex, marriage and family life which I have presented thus far. By contrast with more familiar and romantic views, on which the specialness of sex, marriage and family explains why they are private, I've suggested that rather mundane concerns for bodily integrity, individual agency and equality of rank and status mean that people should be free to form sexual, reproductive and familial associations as seem good to them, rather than as seem good to other people. But this, I've suggested, is not because there's something uniquely important about love, sex and the family, but because treating these matters as private helps to protect people from malice, envy, self-interest and paternalism, thereby promoting their freedom, equality and happiness.

Of course, in comparison with ideas of marriage based on the desire or interest of *parents*, marriages based on romantic affinity and a goal of mutual companionship and support will be egalitarian and liberating. But this does not mean that such ideals of marriage are necessary for democratic forms of family life, let alone that they are sufficient. They are not necessary, because marriages based on instrumental considerations—such as convenience, economy, respectability, the care of children, the farming of land, the running of a successful business—can be as much an advance for equality and liberty over the alternatives as romantic unions. Nor is the romantic ideal of marriage sufficient, because when romance dies some way must still be found to ensure that partners and offspring are provided for.[11]

Democratic forms of privacy, then, may look quite different from those with which we are familiar, or to which we aspire. Companionship, mutual support and sexual fulfilment do not depend on ideals of exclusivity, individuality and of emotional identification characteristic of romantic ideals of the family. For example, shared goals and causes can be just as important to the desire to live together, and may lead people to seek more communal forms of domestic arrangement—such as the kibbutz—or to endorse ideals of 'open' marriage, in which sexual fidelity loses the importance attributed to it on other conceptions of family life. What justifies privacy protection, in other words, is not the number or sex of the people within a marriage, but people's ability to see and treat each other as equals.

A successful marriage is one that is stable, fulfilling and consistent with the freedom and equality of those involved. But how to achieve that is scarcely transparent. By now, it is clear that there is no easy recipe which guarantees success in marriage, in part because there seem to be lots of mutually incompatible ways for people to be happy, comfortable in each others' company, good enough spouses, parents, siblings and children. Plausibly, some of these depend on the free choice of those involved, although our willingness to participate and support a common enterprise does not always depend on our awareness of having chosen it, rather than our perception that it is good and deserves our support. However, the reasons why competent adults are entitled to privacy for their sexual and domestic affairs is not that choice is necessary to success in these—if, indeed, it is—but that it is necessary for us to see and treat each other as equals, rather than as masters and serfs, or as tools lacking ends of their own.

PRIVACY, RIGHTS AND DUTIES

Of course, as the second objection recognises, privacy for sex and family means that matters of collective significance—the size and make-up of the population, the nature of people's desires, their propensity for self-sacrifice, their ability to plan ahead—will be shaped by the cumulative results of lots of individuals' decisions. And it is also true that the results for society as a whole, and for the individuals involved, may be less good than they would have been if they had been planned with a view to maximising these variables.

So, Plato may have been right to believe that private families make people less courageous, energetic and self-sacrificing in collective matters than is desirable, and Tocqueville may have been right to fear that a preoccupation with the wellbeing of our families may lead us to acquiesce in forms of political authority which are paternalistic, bureaucratic and despotic.[12] These possibilities should certainly temper over-enthusiastic celebrations of the value of privacy. Still, the fact that privacy is not costless—that its realisation and protection may prevent us from realising other things of value—does not mean that it is not worth protecting.

Two critical assumptions structure the second complaint about privacy, making it seem plausible that a government of peers is a government in which people lack legitimate interests in privacy. The first assumption is that democratic government cannot be oppressive, because it is government by the people, as well as for the people. However, as Mill noted, experience of democracy quickly teaches people that

> The 'people' who exercise the power, are not always the same people with those over whom it is exercised, and

the 'self-government' spoken of, is not the government of each by himself, but of each by all the rest. The will of the people, moreover, practically means, the will of the most numerous or the most active part of the people; the majority, or those who succeed in making themselves accepted as the majority; the people, consequently, may desire to oppress a part of their number; and precautions are as much needed against this, as against any other abuse of power.[13]

Hence, as Mill argued, constraints on the legal powers of government, and on the hold of popular opinion, are as essential to the freedom, equality and happiness of the members of democratic, as of undemocratic, societies.

The second assumption is that people who are each other's peers in rank are, therefore, essentially similar in their interests, beliefs and ambitions. However, just as government does not cease to be coercive because it is democratic, neither do people's interests and beliefs magically harmonise simply because they are not divided from birth into rulers and ruled. Indeed, democratic freedoms of thought, association and expression can increase differences in people's beliefs, by entitling them to explore their differences, and to shape their social, economic and political life accordingly.

Nonetheless, the second objection to privacy reminds us that the reasons to value privacy are not simply protective. For privacy enables us to take personal, as well as collective, responsibility for our own life and for the lives of other people and, as we will see, the ability to do so is critical to our freedom, equality and wellbeing.

PERSONAL AND COLLECTIVE RESPONSIBILITY

Imagine a world in which we lacked moral or legal entitlements to take personal responsibility for our own lives, or for the lives of other people. It might be a world with individually apportioned tasks, and individual responsibility for fulfilling them, because sometimes this is the best way to achieve common goals. And this world might, and probably would, depend on people showing personal initiative and responsibility, so that collective projects don't grind to a halt, or produce seriously counterproductive results. However, while people might show personal initiative and take personal responsibility for getting things done, in a society where people lack moral and legal *entitlements* to do so, such behaviour would leave them open to censure and punishment by those in authority, and to exposure as a miscreant by those trying to ingratiate themselves with authority in order to 'get ahead'.

Such a society—and its real-life approximations, such as the Soviet Union under Stalin, the People's Republic of China under Mao, Cambodia under the Khmer Rouge, or contemporary North Korea—reminds us of the importance of private initiative and responsibility for the smooth functioning of society, and for economic efficiency. However, our interests in being able to take personal responsibility for our lives, and for those of others, are not only interests in efficiency but in being able to act upon our feelings for other people, our sense of moral and political obligation and, even, our sense of personal destiny or vocation.

It can be of the utmost importance to us not simply *that* our parents, friends and children are cared for, but that *we* are able to care for them, ourselves; not just *that* certain beliefs, ideals, commitments and relationships are recognised and acknowledged, but that *we* are able to recognise and acknowledge them.¹⁴ While we may be willing to pay taxes in order to maintain public hospitals, schools, services and may be very happy to use them all, these are not a substitute for the right to nurse our sick friends and relatives at home, if we can, or to teach our children about their family history, and the geography and history of the countries from which their great-grandparents came. Nor will improved public benefits, however desirable, compensate us for laws that deny us all scope for such things. That is because the ability to take personal responsibility for ourselves and others can be as critical to our wellbeing, freedom and equality as our ability to share in responsibility for joint projects, or to participate in defining the collective goals of our society.

It can sound odd to talk of a 'right to take responsibility', because responsibilities are burdensome, and we very often wish to shirk or avoid them. However, we need only to think of the exclusion of black people from jury service in the USA, or of women from military service in most countries, in order to see that the right to share in collective burdens can be an important civil right. Jury service can be boring and burdensome, and military service can be unpleasant and dangerous. However, it is *stigmatising* to be excluded, whether by custom or by law, from participating in public duties which one is otherwise capable of fulfilling, and this is particularly true when those duties are seen as the obverse of the rights of citizenship.¹⁵

If these points are correct, privacy can reflect our capacities for personal responsibility and initiative, and the importance of being able to identify and fulfil our obligations. There might, after all, be better ways to ensure that parents are cared for in old age than by entitling children to care for their parents; and there might be better ways of ensuring that children are cared for than by entitling parents to look after them. But to deny people the right to offer such care, simply because it might be better provided some other way, would be to ignore the moral importance that such duties have for many, probably most, of us and the political significance of being seen as people capable of fulfilling such duties.

Part of what it is to be a parent, as generally understood, is to care for one's children—to feed, clothe, shelter them, to try and instruct and entertain them, to make them feel loved and happy. So while, the state can rightly require us to educate our children in certain ways, and to contribute to the costs of that education, parents are morally entitled to teach their children about things that they may not learn in school.[16] Likewise, while adult taxpayers are required to contribute towards medical care, housing and pensions for the elderly, democracies also entitle people to look after their parents in their home (so long as they are capable of doing so) and to provide special food, clothing, entertainment and companionship for them.

It is essential to democratic citizenship that people are entitled to act on beliefs, identities and ideals which may have little, if anything, to do with being a citizen and which may, on occasion, conflict with the duties of citizenship. Historically, 'maternal duties' were thought to disqualify women from political participation, and similar arguments were made for members of minority or 'dissenting' religions, as well as for men who had to work for wages in order to support themselves and their families.[17] So it is important to recognise that people's interests in acting on their own behalf, and on behalf of others, have a personal, as well as a collective dimension, and that recognition and protection for both are essential to a democratic conception of privacy.

* * *

In the next chapter we will consider the implications of what we have just learned for the relationship between privacy rights on the one hand, and property rights, on the other. The identification of privacy with private ownership lies behind two different types of objection to privacy. On the one hand, it underpins ideas that privacy rights are redundant, morally and legally, because privacy rights are just property rights in disguise. On the other hand, it underpins complaints that privacy is just a mask for coercive and exploitative relationships, and therefore at odds with democratic freedom, equality and solidarity. But as we will see, privacy-based justifications of private ownership are not always unappealing, and privacy is sometimes promoted, rather than threatened, by collective ownership.

Privacy, Property and Solidarity
Four

We have seen that the value of privacy is both personal and political, a reflection of the importance of personal, as well as collective responsibility, choice and conviction. In so doing, we have shown that privacy can usefully be disaggregated into its component parts, as Judith Thomson claimed in her famous essay on the right to privacy.[1] However, we have described those parts in terms of claims to solitude and seclusion, anonymity and confidentiality, intimacy and family formation, rather than in terms of property ownership and property-like rights over the person—which Thomson favours. We have also seen that our assumptions about the nature and importance of equality profoundly affect the ways we conceptualise people's claims to privacy, and the importance that we attach to those claims. So, on the face of it, privacy seems as closely bound up with our claims to equality and political participation as with property ownership and the rights we have over our body. It is time, then, to look more closely at Thomson's views, and to see what practical, analytical and normative conclusions we can draw from them.

THOMSON'S CRITIQUE OF PRIVACY

Judith Thomson's objections to a moral right to privacy do not arise because she believes that solitude, confidentiality and anonymity are over-rated, or that family life is inseparable from sexual inequality, or a threat to proper patriotism. Rather, her worry is that talk of a moral right to privacy lumps together too many things which, however valuable or important, are best described and justified separately. In particular, she thinks, once we realise how heterogeneous people's claims to privacy are, and reflect on the best way to describe and justify them, we will find that they are really best understood as examples of more basic rights, such as rights to own property, and property-like rights over our bodies, which make it wrong for others to look, listen and touch us without our permission.

Thus, Thomson argues, if she's done something wrong by sneaking into your house and painting your elbows green, what's wrong is that she's invading your *property* and invading your property-like *rights over your body*, which include the right not to have your body looked at, touched, or painted without permission.[2] Similarly, she thinks, deliberate efforts to listen in on arguments with her husband behind closed doors violate her right not to be listened to, although it is not a violation of her rights to stop and get a good earful of the argument if her window is wide open.[3] Leaving the window open, she thinks, can be construed as 'waiving', or giving up, the right not to be overheard; by contrast, she thinks, if she has firmly shut her windows, it should be apparent that she does not want other people to listen to the argument, even if they can catch snatches of it as they walk by.

Likewise, she believes that it is wrong for us to try to get a peep of your wonderful pornographic picture without your permission, because the picture is *yours*—you own it, and one of the rights in which ownership consists is the right to withhold what you own from view.[4] However, if you had been careless enough to leave your picture lying around where anyone can see it, we do not violate your property rights by getting a good look at it, although we may not take it home with us or try to sell it.

So, Thomson supposes, we can describe what is wrong in cases that look like invasions of privacy by reference to other wrongs—wrongful invasions of our rights over our bodies and property. Moreover, she claims, the problem with talk of a right to privacy is not just that all the cases that strike us as violations of a right to privacy can be described at least as well in some other way, but that in none of the cases of privacy violations does it look as though the reason why the violation is wrong is best described by the thought '*because we have a right to privacy*'.[5] However, while Thomson is right that we can sometimes replace talk of privacy with talk of property, or with talk of property-like rights over our bodies, her claim that this is always true rests on fairly controversial assumptions about the nature and content of our moral rights, and there seems no particular reason to accept these.

For example, Thomson assumes that we have a right not to be looked at, which we always waive when we go out in public.[6] Hence, for Thomson, there is no need to invoke a right to privacy in order to explain why you have a right not to be looked at by intruders peeping through your windows, although you have no right not to be looked at as you go strolling down the street. Yet Stanley Benn seems correct to distinguish a casual glance by a passer-by—which, he agrees with Thomson, does not violate our privacy—and a fixed or pervasive stare which might do so. As Benn says, 'there is a difference between happening to be seen and having someone closely observe, and perhaps record, what one is doing, even in a public place'.[7] These differences are essential to recent debates on the ethics of using closed circuit television (CCTV) in public places, as well as the use of global positioning systems (GPS) and facial recognition technologies, not only because such technologies can themselves foster insecurity, violence and discrimination, but because they may also violate our claims to privacy in public.[8]

In assessing Thomson's thesis, then, a great deal turns on how we understand the precise contours of our moral rights, and what we assume counts as waiving, or relinquishing those rights.[9] The difficulty, however, is that our conceptions of property ownership and of rights over our bodies do not seem to have the sharpness which Thomson assumes—their precise extent, weight and justification, for instance, seem much less clear than she supposes. Thus, many of us would agree with Thomson that it is bad manners, but not a rights-violation to listen to her argument with her husband, if she forgot to shut the window. Nonetheless, we may still believe that we would violate her rights if we treated that open French window as an invitation to step inside and help ourselves to her philosophy library—or just to sit in a chair for a quick read of one of her books.

We presume that open French windows do not constitute waived rights against uninvited visitors, or over-enthusiastic philosophers, because the right to prevent others from entering our homes is of so much greater importance than the right not to be overheard. People therefore need to be able to air their rooms without worrying that they will be thought to have given up these rights if they forget to shut their windows or doors. Hence, our ideas about what counts as waiving a right depend, in part, on the importance of the right we are considering as well as, most likely, on the typical harms which it seeks to avert, and the circumstances in which it is typically claimed.

Once we take these points on board, it becomes much less clear that we will illuminate, rather than complicate, life by replacing talk of privacy rights with talk of property ownership and property-like rights over our bodies. More troubling, however, is the possibility that replacing talk of privacy with talk of liberty, property and bodily integrity actually *confuses* us about what people are claiming, and with what justification.

Compare, for example, the two different bones of contention between Joyce Maynard and J. D. Salinger. The first one concerned Maynard's desire to publish an account of their life together in her autobiographical work, *At Home in the World*. Publication clearly entailed a loss of privacy for Salinger, but he was scarcely claiming that his property rights were at stake: nor could he, as there are no property rights in a shared history as a couple, or in ordinary experience. Maynard, of course, was claiming that she had a right to publish her own experience, to publicise her privacy, even though doing so inevitably meant publicising some of Salinger's as well. Books are objects of property and, like any writer, Maynard must have hoped that her book would sell well and bring her wealth, as well as fame. But it does not follow that her interests in publishing were primarily financial, rather than expressive, or that to treat her claims to publicise her privacy as claims to profit from her property would adequately capture her interests, either.

By contrast, Maynard's interests in selling the letters Salinger wrote to her were financial: and her interests in the letters were as a form of property, rather than as a record of a shared experience, or of insight into Salinger's feelings, activities and character. Salinger was unable to prevent the sale of the letters, but he succeeded in persuading a court that, as their author, no one should have the right to publish their contents without his permission. The interests that Salinger sought to protect, then, were interests in confidentiality rather than in financial gain, and his aim in asserting his property rights over the letters was to prevent their publication, rather than to ensure himself a share of the profits that publication would generate.

It is helpful, then, rather than obfuscatory, to say that the interests Salinger sought to vindicate were interests in *privacy*, rather than *ownership*, although the right to prevent publication without consent can be financially desirable. Indeed, it is more helpful to note that his interests were in *privacy* rather than *liberty*, as it was only the freedom to prevent publication of the letters that interested him, rather than other freedoms, such as freedoms of expression, association or participation. The point for Salinger, in other words, was not that he wanted to be *consulted*, or to *participate* in choosing publishers, formats, editors and the like, but that he wanted to *prevent any publication at all*. Referring to Salinger's interests as interests in *privacy* conveys that idea fairly readily, because interests in confidentiality are so central to most understandings of privacy. By contrast, they are very much less central to ideas of liberty, which is why replacing talk of privacy with talk of liberty in this case is likely to be confusing, if not actually misleading.

PRIVACY AND COLLECTIVE PROPERTY

Claims to privacy, then, are not reducible to claims to personal property, and this has implications for the way we approach public policy, not just philosophical analysis. We have seen that one difficulty with trying to translate people's claims to privacy into claims to property ownership is that ownership consists in a bundle of rights which can be disaggregated and parcelled out in different ways. So, if I own a car or a house it is typically not the case that I can let them disintegrate if it suits me to do so, because there are a variety of regulations which will come into force should I leave my car to rust on the street, or let my house fall into disrepair.

This is not because someone else owns my house and car, merely that in these cases (and others like them), my ownership does not include the right to destroy my property through neglect. On the other hand, if I rent a house or a car I will not have the right to sell them or to give them away, but I will have the right to use them and, for the duration of my lease, to exclude their owner from using them. So while it is true that my property rights may well protect my privacy, replacing talk of privacy with talk of property rights is unlikely to improve the clarity or precision of our ideas, because there are so many different, sometimes incompatible, types of property.[10]

Some forms of property are held on behalf of a group of people, such as a family or a group of investors, or even a nation. Such property is often called 'collective property' to highlight the fact that ownership rights are supposed to be used on behalf of a group of people, rather than a single individual, and to be exercised either by some representative of the group of owners, or by the members of that group acting jointly. Other forms of property are called 'private property', meaning that they are held by a person, or on behalf of a person, who is free to exercise his or her rights of ownership without consulting others.

It seems natural to suppose we should prefer private to collective property if we value privacy, but such an assumption is mistaken. True, some forms of collective property can be quite invasive of privacy, as these typically mean that all owners are entitled to a say in their disposition. This is notoriously the case with those New York apartment blocks which are cooperatively owned (even though the individual apartments are owned privately), because fellow owners are entitled to a good deal of information about would-be-buyers in order to decide whether to approve or veto any sales.

However, not all forms of collective property are like that. State-owned and -run housing, for example, may be less privacy-invasive than private housing, because the information required in order to obtain a lease is typically held by people with whom one has less contact than with private landlords. So, even if the quantity of information one has to divulge is no smaller or less intimate, the different ways that this information is typically held, and the different people who typically hold it, mean that one may actually have more, rather than less, privacy as a renter of state-owned, rather than privately owned property.

Because private property ownership is not synonymous with privacy, the privatisation of public space and of public property can threaten, rather than promote, privacy. For many of us, living in cramped and crowded conditions—or with noisy neighbours and families—public gardens, squares, parks, libraries and museums are places where we can go for a bit of peace and quiet, or for a 'private chat' or heart-to-heart with our friends. When such places are free of charge, as well as open to the public, they provide much-needed opportunities for solitude, anonymity and time together with friends and lovers, as well as fresh air, culture and entertainment. Hence, the creation of public facilities such as libraries, sports centres, youth centres, parks and gardens can create opportunities for privacy where, previously, these were few and far between.

The importance of public space for privacy is highlighted by a poignant essay on homelessness by the philosopher and legal scholar, Jeremy Waldron.[11] One way of describing the plight of a homeless person is to say that

> there is no place governed by a private property rule where he is allowed to be whenever *he* chooses, no place governed by a private property rule from which he may not at any time be excluded as a result of someone else's say-so. . . . For the most part, the homeless are excluded from *all* places governed by private property rules, whereas the rest of us are, in the same sense, excluded from *all but one* (or maybe all but a few) of those places.

Hence, in a world where all collective property was privatised, or where no collective property—such as streets, parks, subways, shelters—was available for the homeless to attend to their needs, the freedom of the homeless 'would depend utterly on the forbearance of those who owned the places that made up the territory of the society in question'.

It matters fundamentally to the privacy of the homeless, therefore, that there be forms of collective property—such as the generous provision of public lavatories, and public baths—which are available for them to conduct activities such as sleeping, eating and urinating. These activities are 'both urgent and quotidian', as Waldron puts it, because a person simply cannot wait to perform them until s/he has acquired a home or some private property. So, whatever else it is that we owe to those who are homeless, Waldron argues, we owe them places where they may legally fulfil their needs discreetly in public.[12]

PRIVACY AND PRIVATE PROPERTY

We have seen that claims to privacy cannot be reduced to claims to property ownership. But this does not meant that the nature and value of privacy are irrelevant to what we are entitled to own, and what we are entitled to do with our property. If, on the one hand, it means that public property may be used for private purposes such as conversations, education, fitness, cleanliness and shelter, on the other hand our interests in confidentiality, in anonymity, intimacy and domesticity help to explain why people should be entitled to some forms of private property, even if they are able to meet their needs for food, clothing and shelter through the use of property that is held in common.

If privacy is valuable it seems desirable, and perhaps even necessary, that people should have some forms of property which they can treat as seems good to them. For example, the idea of making a personal sacrifice not only of one's time but also of one's comfort and possessions means that we must be able to hand over—even destroy ceremonially—something that one would otherwise be entitled to use for oneself. Likewise, if gifts are to be capable of expressing an appreciation of the particularity of another—whether that involves recognition of their needs as a student, a newly-wed, a parent, or of their talents, hobbies and tastes—it is important that our gifts are capable of expressing something about the giver, as well as the receiver. They may be mass-produced or handmade, cheap or expensive, but if they are successfully to serve the communicative purposes of the giver, people must have a fair bit of scope in their selection, and in the timing of their presentation.

The importance of these social, rather than financial, interests in private property is well brought out by Wolff and de-Shalit's study of disadvantage.[13] As they say, 'Being able to care for others is part of being a person, at least under normal conditions, and therefore part of one's well-being', and an important expression of this ability to care is the desire to reciprocate kindness, and to show gratitude for the kindness of others. As Wolff and de-Shalit explain, 'Showing gratitude to others, "paying one's respects", and showing joy at other people's joy all form part of a flourishing human life.'

However, people may find themselves unable adequately to undertake the socially accepted acts that express their gratitude and joy because they are too poor, as well as because they suffer from physical disabilities. 'Doing good to others allows one self-esteem. Being human means not only to receive; one wants to give', the authors were told by one of their interviewees; and the sense of humiliation and loss of honour that comes with the inability to express one's respect or love is so powerful, and so widespread across individuals and cultures, that Wolff and de-Shalit conclude that it constitutes a morally significant form of disadvantage.

Strictly speaking none of this requires a set of private property rights of the sort with which we are familiar. We could instead imagine some sort of store house (or set of store houses, spread around like cinemas and pubs) to which people could go and, in exchange for the promise of a certain number of hours of work, either there or elsewhere, could choose an object which they could then use as a gift or keep for themselves. This would still require people to have considerable discretion in when, how and why they use their time, as well as assuming that they are entitled to exchange their time for objects which they can use as they please.

However, this sort of arrangement would not enable us to give gifts which are personal in the sense of being objects which had belonged to us, been used by us, or been made by us. Nor would it mean that we would have access, ourselves, to objects whose use may be functional, but which also have emotional and symbolic significance for us. So, thinking about this example illuminates the significance of forms of ownership that enable us to keep, use, lend and give away things that are ours, in the sense of having been a part of our lives, as an expression of our particular beliefs, attachments and ideals.

Private ownership is not just about the right to use objects such as clothes, beds and furniture, or to feed ourselves and our loved ones. Rather, it is about the ability to find forms of these that suit us, and respond to our particular beliefs and needs, tastes and temperaments. As Iris Marion Young says, 'an important aspect of the value of privacy is the ability to have a dwelling space of one's own . . . in which one lives among the things that help support the narrative of one's life'.[14] So, it looks as though the value of privacy justifies some forms of private, as well as collective, property.

* * *

We have seen that Thomson is wrong to treat claims to privacy as though they are just claims to property in disguise. Granted that both the value of privacy and the moral right to privacy will likely overlap with other values and rights, we have seen that talk of privacy can illuminate the importance of specific liberties and specific goods and bads that we might otherwise overlook or misinterpret. An implication of this is that privacy is not the threat to economic equality which is sometimes supposed, even though it will sometimes justify us in creating forms of property that are private rather than public.

There are two main reasons for this. The first is that the value of privacy is unlikely to justify the creation, maintenance and control of significant personal wealth and economic power. Though people's interests in solitude, intimacy and family life are both various and competitive—since we cannot all get what we want when we want it—there is nothing about the nature or importance of these interests which suggests that societies should be indifferent to concentrations of wealth and power, or to significant differences in people's life chances consequent on the ownership of different amounts of property. Justifications of private property based on the value of *privacy* then, do not commit us to any substantive theses about the best way to organise the production and exchange of goods, the virtues of competition, or the benefits of a free market in general, or in particular.

Second, it is important to remember that what counts as a legitimate object of property, as well as what counts as a morally permissible way to acquire and use that property, depends on the assumptions we make about the moral status of people, of animals, of natural resources and of human labour. So justifications of collective or state-run property will not be democratic if minorities can be enslaved, if prisoners can be turned into indentured servants or if the labour of women is valued at less—economically, politically, morally—than the labour of men. That is why, when thinking about the value of privacy relative to other values, and the respective content and justification of privacy rights relative to other rights, it is important to be clear about the *political* assumptions involved.

Talk about privacy then, is not pointless or simply confused. However, the reasons why it is not highlight the importance of politics to morality. Although it seems that we can explore the nature and value of privacy without worrying about the justification for different types of government, we have seen that this is a mistake. It is a mistake because the value we attribute to privacy depends, fundamentally, on how we conceive people's interests, circumstances and prospects, and for this we need to make some assumptions about the power that they have relative to others. Hence, privacy is a deeply political value, inextricably connected to the ways we conceive ourselves as individuals and as members of society.

Unfortunately, in this short book I have paid scant attention to the international dimensions of privacy, or to the way that travel, trade, immigration and war affect the ways we can describe and evaluate it. The international dimensions of domestic politics have become ever more important, and this affects the ways we can conceptualise and evaluate claims to privacy, given its consequences for people's identities, relationships, liberties and obligations. The value of privacy, therefore, has an international as well as national and personal dimension, which merits philosophical consideration. But we must leave that for another day.

Conclusion

Is privacy valuable? The answer, we have seen, is 'yes', although it is not always easy to describe and evaluate privacy, or to determine its likely consequences for ourselves and others. Proponents of privacy believe that it promotes people's freedom, equality, and happiness, whereas sceptics worry that it leaves the weak and vulnerable at the mercy of the powerful. We have seen that there is some truth in each of these seemingly inconsistent claims. Protections for privacy are not costless, and may sometimes prevent us from speaking our mind, learning from others, or acting as we should. Moreover, the likely consequences of privacy for people's freedom, equality and happiness depend on how we describe and evaluate the latter. Hence, some ways of thinking about privacy place it on a collision course with the freedom of women and their equality with men, although there is nothing intrinsic to privacy which means that it must have such effects. Conversely, privacy can help to protect people from unjustified scorn, humiliation and recrimination, as well as from bribery and coercion, although there is nothing inevitable about this, either.

We cannot describe the nature and value of privacy without making complex, often implicit, assumptions about the ways of the world, and our place within it. If these assumptions are mistaken, it is likely that our ideas about privacy will be mistaken, too. If these assumptions are at odds with the claims of ordinary people to govern themselves, then our ideas about privacy are very likely to promote beliefs, desires, habits and relationships which unjustifiably elevate the interests of a favoured few over the unfortunate many, and which treat the trivial failings of the latter with great severity while leaving the vices and crimes of the former unchecked and unpunished. If, instead, we try to resolve disputes about privacy in light of our best assumptions about people's interests, rights and duties in self-government, we stand some chance of describing privacy in a way that reflects their interests in freedom, equality and happiness.

However, realising that chance depends on what we do, as well as what we think. If it is unlikely that privacy will be valuable unless we describe it in ways that reflect our values, so it is unlikely that it will be valuable unless we try to make it so. This is not because all values are relative—though there is, inevitably, a comparative aspect to what we value. Rather, it is because the world is not impervious to human desires, human beliefs and human actions, although it is not completely amenable to them, either. What we think and do, then, can change the value of privacy for ourselves and others and that seems a fitting thought on which to end our sketch of privacy if we are interested in 'thinking in action'.

Notes

INTRODUCTION

1 See, for example, this oft-quoted line from the Younger Report on privacy: 'One of the obstacles to the development of a satisfactory law of privacy has been the difficulty of definition.' Kenneth Younger, Chairman, *Report of the Committee on Privacy*, Cmnd 5012. Para 37, p. 10. HMSO (London, 1972).

2 Daphne Joyce Maynard published *At Home in the World* in 1998, which described the 10 months, in 1972, when she had lived with Salinger.

3 Judith Jarvis Thomson, 'The Right to Privacy,' in *Philosophical Dimensions of Privacy: An Anthology*, ed. Ferdinand D. Schoeman (Cambridge University Press, 1984), pp. 272–290.

4 The effort to 'refute' Thomson shapes most of the philosophical literature on privacy. See Anita Allen's *Uneasy Access: Privacy for Women in a Free Society* (Rowman and Littlefield, New Jersey, 1988); Julie C. Inness' *Privacy, Intimacy and Isolation* (Oxford University Press, 1992). Judith Wagener DeCew provides a helpful guide to these debates in *In Pursuit of Privacy: Law, Ethics and the Rise of Technology* (Cornell University Press, Ithaca, NY, 1997) and in her entry on privacy for the *Stanford Encyclopedia of Philosophy*, which is free and can be found on-line at http://plato.stanford.edu.

5 Alexis de Tocqueville's wonderful *Democracy in America* is readily available, in many different editions, and can be found free on the internet at www.gutenberg.org/files/815/815-h/815-h.htm.

6 Aristotle's *Politics* Book I, Sections 3–7.

7 Robert Nozick, *Anarchy, State and Utopia* (Basic Books, New York, 1974), p. 331. For an excellent explanation and evaluation of Nozick's views on liberty, and their connection to his ideas about property ownership, taxation and equality, see Jonathan Wolff's *Robert Nozick: Property, Justice and the Minimal State* (Polity Press, London, 1991).

8 For a helpful discussion of Bentham's critique of the idea of moral rights, and extracts from Bentham's *Anarchical Fallacies*, see Jeremy Waldron's

Nonsense Upon Stilts: Bentham, Burke and Marx on the Rights of Man (Routledge, London, 2009).

ONE PRIVACY AND DEMOCRACY

1. Stanley I. Benn, 'Privacy, Freedom and Respect for Persons', in *Philosophical Dimensions of Privacy: An Anthology*, ed. Ferdinand D. Schoeman (Cambridge University Press, 1984), pp. 223–244; and Jeffrey H. Reiman, 'Privacy, Intimacy and Personhood', pp. 300–316 in the same volume.
2. James Rachels, 'Why Privacy is Important', in ed. Schoeman, pp. 290–299.
3. Thomas Nagel's essay 'Concealment and Exposure', first published in the journal *Philosophy and Public Affairs*, is also available in a collection of essays and book reviews, many of which are concerned with issues of privacy, called *Concealment and Exposure and Other Essays* (Oxford University Press, 2002).
4. In addition to his essay, 'Concealment and Exposure', readers may be interested in his on-line debate in *Slate* with the American journalist Michael Kinsley, sparked by the 'Monica Lewinsky Affair', or US president Clinton's sex life, at www.slate.com/id/3627.
5. Sue Mendus criticises Nagel's view of the public/private distinction in 'Private Faces in Public Places', in *The Legacy of H. L. A Hart: Legal, Political and Moral Philosophy*, eds Matthew Kramer, Claire Grant, Ben Colburn, and Antony Hatzistavrou (Oxford University Press, Oxford, 2008), pp. 299–315.
6. Jeffrey H. Reiman, 'Privacy, Intimacy and Personhood', in ed. Schoeman, p. 310.
7. For Mill's passionate defence of the importance of 'freedom of tastes and pursuits', see ch. 3 on individuality in his wonderful short book, *On Liberty*. This can be found in different scholarly editions, and is available for free on-line at www.bartleby.com/130/.
8. Catharine A. MacKinnon, *Feminism Unmodified: Discourses on Life and Law* (Harvard University Press, Cambridge, MA, 1987), p. 101.
9. First published in 1928, Virginia Woolf's little book is readily available, as is her essay *Three Guineas*, published in 1938, mocking the institutions of higher education, church and army from which women were excluded, but which still eagerly solicited women's financial support.
10. I develop this argument in more detail in 'Must Privacy and Equality Conflict? A Philosophical Examination of Some Legal Evidence', *Social Research: An International Quarterly of the Social Sciences* 67.4. (Winter 2000): 1137–1171; 'Feminism, Democracy and the Right to Privacy', *Minerva* 9. (November 2005) available at www.mic.ul.ie/stephen/vol9/Feminism.

pdf; and 'Privacy Rights and Democracy: A Contradiction in Terms?' *Contemporary Political Theory* 5.2. (May 2006): 142–162.
11 For an alternative way of approaching the role of privacy in a democratic society see Corey Brettschneider's *Democratic Rights: The Substance of Self-Government* (Princeton University Press, Princeton, NJ, 2007), ch. 4. My main difficulty with this interesting and important book is that its view of democracy seems excessively American and liberal, with its emphasis on the values of political autonomy, equality of interests and reciprocity, and American debates on the constitutional right to privacy.
12 Those interested in Mill's ideas on the secret ballot, and on politics more generally, may want to look at Nadia Urbinati's *Mill on Democracy: From the Athenian Polis to Representative Government* (University of Chicago Press, 2002). Mill's views on the secret ballot can be found in ch. 10 of his *Considerations on Representative Government*.
13 Geoffrey Brennan and Philip Pettit, 'Unveiling the Vote', *British Journal of Political Science* 20.32 (July 1990): 311–333.
14 See http://en.wikipedia.org/wiki/Perp_walk and for the debate over the treatment of Dominique Strauss-Khan, the former head of the IMF, see www.poznter.org/latestnews/als_morning-meeting/132692/is-it-ethical-to-use-perp-walk-images-of dominique-strauss-khan-imf-chief-accused-of-attempted-rape/.

TWO PRIVACY, EQUALITY AND FREEDOM OF EXPRESSION

1 An example of this can be seen in Richard Mohr's view that 'To lose a child in a custody case for prejudicial reasons [i.e. because of prejudice against homosexuality] is, to be sure, to suffer an indignity'—which seems like a breathtakingly inadequate description of one potential harm of outing. See Mohr's *Gay Ideas: Outing and Other Controversies* (Beacon Press, Boston, 1992), p. 34.
2 See, for example, 'The Threat to Our Press' by Paul Dacre, *Guardian*, 10 November 2008, at www.guardian.co.uk/media/2008/nov/10/paul-dacre-press-threats.
3 For example, there is no reason to think that your claims to form a sports group should depend on showing that churches, workplaces, etc. do not organise sports events—nor on the claim that it would be impossible for them to do so. In short, people should not have to make implausible claims for the uniqueness, merits and need of their associations in order to be free to join with others on some common project. See W. L. Weinstein's 'The Private and the Free: A Conceptual

Inquiry', in J. Chapman and R. Pennock (eds) *Privacy: Nomos XIII* (Atherton Press, New York, 1971), footnote 29, p. 47.

4 See 'The Right to Privacy (The Implicit made Explicit)' by Samuel D. Warren and Louis D. Brandeis, originally published in the *Harvard Law Review*, and reprinted in *Philosophical Dimensions of Privacy: An Anthology*, ed. Ferdinand D. Schoeman (Cambridge University Press, 2007), pp. 75–103.

5 The quotation comes from Mill's *On Liberty*, ch. 4, 'Of the Limits to the Authority of Society Over the Individual'. The complete text of *On Liberty* is available free of charge on the web, but there are some excellent scholarly editions which can be easily bought.

6 Stanley Benn: 'To treat even an entertainer's life simply as material for entertainment is to pay no more regard to him as a person than to an animal in a menagerie.' 'Privacy, Freedom and Respect for Persons', in ed. Schoeman, pp. 223–244, at 233.

7 The details can be found at http://en.wikipedia.org/wiki/Sara_Keays #Parkinson.27s_resignation.

8 See, for example, http://news.bbc.co.uk/1/hi/health/5118166.stm and http://news.bbc.co.uk/1/hi/health/1803609.stm.

9 *The Financial Times*, 30 July 2008, p. 12: 'Judgement Call: Four Professionals Offer Expert Advice: Do Investors Have a Right to Know About a CEO's Illness?' My sense is that it is not just investors who need to know, but investment professionals and, indeed, those working for the company.

10 Newspapers have an interest in paying as little for these stories as possible; so it seems unnecessary, as well as undesirable to make it illegal for newspapers to pay people to publish these sorts of stories about their lives, even if payment is likely to increase their supply and, thus, the invasions of privacy which they involve.

11 www.guardian.co.uk/media/2010/apr/10/newspapers-phone-hacking-inquiry. On 3 October 2010, the *News of the World* printed an apology to Vanessa Perroncel for invading her private life, and accepted that its claims that she had had an affair with the footballer John Terry were untrue, at www.guardian.co.uk/media/greenslade/2010/oct/07/ newsoftheworld-john-terry.

12 For a helpful discussion of privacy for politicians—and one which pays attention to questions of power and responsibility within different government bodies and administrative agencies – see Dennis F. Thompson's *Political Ethics and Public Office* (Harvard University Press, Cambridge, MA, 1987), ch. 5.

THREE PRIVACY: THE FAMILY, SEX AND REPRODUCTION

1 For presentations and discussion of these criticisms see Catherine MacKinnon, *Feminism Unmodified* (Harvard University Press, Cambridge, MA, 1987); Susan Moller Okin's *Justice, Gender and the Family* (Basic Books, New York, 1989), especially chapters 6 and 7, pp. 110–169; Jean L. Cohen, *Regulating Intimacy: A New Legal Paradigm* (Princeton University Press, Princeton, NJ, 2002).

2 The key phrase comes from Sir Edward Coke's *The Institutes of the Laws of England*, 1628: 'For a man's home is his castle, *et domus sua cuique est tutissimum refugium* [and each man's home is his safest refuge]'. This was given more poetic expression by Pitt the Elder: 'The Poorest man may in his cottage bid defiance to all the forces of the crown. It may be frail—its roof may shake—the wind may blow through it—the storm may enter—the rain may enter—but the King of England cannot enter'!

3 See Mary Lyndon Shanley's 'Just Marriage: On the Public Importance of Private Unions', in *Just Marriage*, eds Joshua Cohen and Deborah Chasman (Oxford University Press, 2004), part I, which, in addition to Shanley's article for the *Boston Review*, contains responses by several distinguished writers.

4 For more details, see Stephen Cretney's fascinating book, *Law, Law Reform and the Family* (Oxford University Press, 1998), pp. 180–183.

5 For examples of this controversy applied to the issue of euthanasia, otherwise known as 'assisted suicide', see Ronald Dworkin, *Life's Dominion: An Argument about Abortion, Euthanasia and Individual Freedom* (Vintage Press, New York, 1994), especially chapters 7 and 8. See also 'The Philosophers' Brief', an open letter on euthanasia, published in the *New York Review of Books*. This is available on-line, with follow-up letters at www.nybooks.com/articles/archives/1997/mar/27/assisted-suicide-the-philosophers-brief/.

6 Joshua Cohen, 'Privacy, Pluralism and Democracy', in his *Philosophy, Politics, Democracy: Selected Essays* (Harvard University Press, Cambridge, MA, 2009), p. 316. Or as Ferdinand Schoeman says, 'Privacy involves norms that allow the pursuit and development of aims and relationships that count simply because the people involved find meaning in them', in his essay 'Privacy and Intimate Information', p. 416 of his edited collection, *Philosophical Dimensions of Privacy* (Cambridge University Press, 1984).

7 See Matthew W. Finkin's Piper Lecture of 1996, published as 'Employee Privacy, American Values and the Law' in the *Chicago-Kent Law Review* 72. (1996–7): 221–269, and his 'Some Further Thoughts on the Usefulness of Comparativism in the Law of Employee Privacy', in *Employee Rights and*

Employment Policy Journal 14. (2010): 11–53, with the discussion of the more recent cases of *Jespersen v. Harrah's Operating Co., Inc.*, 444 F. 3d 1104 (9th Cir. 2006) and *Ellis v. United Parcel Service, Inc.*, 523 F. 3d 823 (7th Cir. 2008). The former case concerned a female bartender who was fired when she refused to wear make-up. The latter case concerned a United Parcel Service manager who was fired when it was discovered that he had a long relationship with, and had eventually married, someone working in a different unit of the postal service, thereby contravening the company's blanket ban on 'fraternization'. See also Barbara Ehrenreich's *Nickel and Dimed: Undercover in Low-Wage USA*, recently republished by Granta, UK, 2010.

8 These examples come from Finkin 1996–7, pp. 226–227, 238–239, 241–242.

9 For an extension of this argument in response to American laws on employee dismissal, see Matthew W. Finkin, 'Discharge and Disgrace: A Comment on the "Urge To Treat People As Objects"', in *Employee Rights and Employment Policy Journal* 1.1. (Fall 1997): 1–23. Why, Finkin asks, should we 'allow employers to treat people, even the morally miscreant, as public "object lessons"' for others? (at 22).

10 The United States Senate has recently ratified a law enabling homosexual men and women openly to serve in the military. See www.nytimes.com/2010/12/23/us/politics/23military.html?_r=1&scp=3&sq=don't%20ask,%20don't%20tell&st=cse.

11 Jean Bethke Elshtain's *Public Man, Private Woman*, ch. 6 (Princeton University Press, Princeton, NJ, 1993), pp. 298–354; and Nancy L. Rosenblum's *Another Liberalism: Romanticism and the Reconstruction of Liberal Thought* (Harvard University Press, Cambridge, MA, 1987).

12 Plato's *Republic*, Book V contains the argument that the Guardians, or group protecting society, should have no private property and no families of their own, so as not to distract them from the common good. *The Republic* can be found free on-line, as well as in numerous scholarly and edited versions. Alexis de Tocqueville, *Democracy in America*, vol. 2, ch. 6, 'What Sort of Despotism Democratic Nations Have to Fear'. Of the modern citizen, he thinks, 'Each one of them, withdrawn into himself, is almost unaware of the fate of the rest. Mankind, for him, consists in his children and his personal friends. As for the rest of his fellow citizens, they are near enough, but he does not notice them. He touches them but feels nothing. He exists in and for himself, and though he still may have a family, one can at least say that he has not got a fatherland'. (Tocqueville 1966, p. 692).

13 The quotation comes from the opening pages of *On Liberty*, ch. 1, 'Introductory'.
14 As Ferdinand Schoeman says, 'Without an individual's capacity to create value in something by valuing it, what we are left with is respect for values but no respect for persons as such', in his 'Privacy and Intimate Information', p. 414.
15 The following Supreme Court cases help to illustrate the point: *Batson v. Kentucky*, 476 U.S. 79 (1986), concerning the exclusion of blacks from jury duty; and *J.E.B. v. Alabama ex rel.* T.B., 511 U.S. 127 (1994), concerning the exclusion of women.
16 For those interested in these issues, Harry Brighouse's *On Education* (*Thinking in Action*), in this series, may be helpful (Routledge, 2006), as well as Matthew Clayton's *Justice and Legitimacy in Upbringing* (Oxford University Press, 2006), and Adam Swift's polemical, but thought-provoking, *How Not to Be a Hypocrite: School Choice for the Morally Perplexed* (Routledge, 2003).
17 See, for example, Carole Pateman's 'The Patriarchical Welfare State', and the other fascinating essays in *Democracy and the Welfare State*, ed. Amy Gutmann, (Princeton University Press, Princeton, NJ, 1988); Nancy Fraser's 'Women, Welfare and the Politics of Need Interpretation' in her book *Unruly Practices: Power, Discourse and Gender in Contemporary Social Theory* (Polity Press, Bristol, UK, 1989) ch. 7, pp. 144–160; and Mary Daly and Katherine Rake's *Gender and the Welfare State: Care and Welfare in Europe and the USA* (Polity Press, Bristol, UK, 2003). In *American Citizenship: The Quest for Inclusion* Judith Shklar reflected on the importance that the free labour/slave labour distinction had for subsequent American conceptions of race, labour, citizenship and welfare (Harvard University Press, Cambridge, MA, 1995).

FOUR PRIVACY, PROPERTY AND SOLIDARITY

1 Judith Jarvis Thomson, 'The Right to Privacy', in *Philosophical Dimensions of Privacy: An Anthology*, ed. Ferdinand D. Schoeman (Cambridge University Press, 1984), pp. 272–289. This article was originally published in the journal *Philosophy and Public Affairs* 4. (1975): 295–314, and has been anthologised many times since, including in a wonderful collection of Thomson's essays called *Rights, Restitution and Risk: Essays in Moral Theory*, edited by William Parent (Harvard University Press, Cambridge, MA, 1986).
2 See p. 279:

> it's a nasty business to damage a knee; but you've a right to damage yours, and certainly nobody else has—its being your left knee

includes your having the right that nobody else but you shall damage it. And, as I think, it also includes your having the right that nobody else shall touch it or look at it.

Summarising her view, Thomson says (p. 280):

> These rights—the right not to be looked at and the right to not be listened to—are analogous to rights we have over our property. It sounds funny to say we have such rights. They are not mentioned when we give lists of rights. . . . These un-grand rights seem to be closely enough akin to be worth grouping together under one heading. For lack of a better term, I shall simply speak of 'the right over the person', a right which I shall take to consist of the un-grand rights I mentioned, and others as well.

3 Thomson p. 273 for the contrast between the loud fight and the quiet fight behind closed doors.
4 Thomson, p. 287: "Someone looks at your pornographic picture in your wall-safe? He violates your right that your belongings not be looked at, and you have that right because you have ownership rights—and it is because you have them that what he does is wrong."
5 Thomson, pp. 286–287:

> The fact, supposing it is a fact, that every right in the right to privacy cluster is also in some other right cluster does not by itself show that the right to privacy is in any plausible sense a 'derivative' right. A more important point seems to me to be this: the fact that we have a right to privacy does not explain our having any of the rights in the right to privacy cluster. . . . That we feel the need to find something in common to all of the rights in the cluster and, moreover, feel we haven't yet got it in the very fact that they *are* all in the cluster, is a consequence of our feeling that one cannot explain our having any of the rights in the cluster in the words: 'Because we have a right to privacy'.

(emphasis in the original)

But while I agree with Thomson that we have a right against torture, I do not see that this shows we do not have a right to privacy *too*, which would *also* be violated if we were tortured to extract personal information. The same act can be wrong for a variety of reasons, and violate a variety of rights. It is therefore possible that being tortured to extract personal information is worse than being tortured to affirm or negate some statement of scientific or political fact, because in some cases of torture the violation of privacy would constitute an *additional* and very significant part of the wrong, as it would not if the personal information were of no particular significance to you or to your torturers.

6 Page 285:

> it seems to me that if you do go out in public, you waive your right to not be photographed and looked at. But of course you . . . have a right to be free of . . . annoyance in public places; so in particular, you have a right that the photographers and crowds not press in too closely

just because they are desperate to get a look, or a 'shot' of you. The issue of whether celebrities can legally be photographed without their consent while going about their daily life is one of the most controversial issues in UK and EU law. Since *von Hannover v. Germany*—where Princess Caroline of Monaco won a case of this sort—it looks as though European law will follow the stricter French perspective in these matters than the more lax German and UK ones. See *Privacy and the Press*, Joshua Rozenberg (Oxford University Press, 2004). Rozenberg laments the decision in the Princess Caroline case, pp. xiii–iv. See also www.rozenberg.net.

7 Benn, 'Privacy, freedom and respect for persons', in *Philosophical Dimensions of Privacy: An Anthology*, ed. Ferdinand D. Schoeman (Cambridge University Press, 1984), p. 225.

8 See Mark Tunick, 'Privacy in Public Places: Do GPS and Video Surveillance Provide Plain Views?' in *Social Theory and Practice* 35. 4. (Oct. 2009): 597–622; Jesper Ryberg, 'Privacy Rights, Crime Prevention, CCTV and the Life of Mrs. Aremac', in *Res Publica* 13. 2. (2007): 127–143; and the responses by Annabelle Lever, 'Mrs. Aremac and the Camera,' and Benjamin Goold, 'The Difference Between Lonely Old Ladies and CCTV Cameras', in *Res Publica* 14. (2008): 35–42, 43–47. On facial recognition technologies see Christopher S. Milligan, 'Facial Recognition Technology, Video Surveillance and Privacy', *Southern Califronia Interdisciplinary Law Journal* 9. (1999): 295–33.

9 Thomson, 'The Right to Privacy', p. 278, for example. It should be noted that this article is very old—it was written in 1975. For those interested in the more developed versions of Thomson's theory of rights, see the following collections of her essays: *Rights, Restitution and Risk: Essays* (Harvard University Press, Cambridge, MA, 1986); and *The Realm of Rights* (Harvard University Press, Cambridge, MA, 1990).

10 Those interested in recent debates in the philosophy of property may want to look at Stephen R. Munzer's *A Theory of Property* (Cambridge

University Press, Cambridge, 1990), John P. Christman's *The Myth of Property: Toward an Egalitarian Theory of Ownership* (Oxford University Press, Oxford, 1994) and G. A. Cohen's *Self-Ownership, Freedom and Equality* (Cambridge University Press, Cambridge, 1995), which are efforts to understand, evaluate and then revise from an egalitarian perspective, traditional views of property.

11 'Homelessness and the Issue of Freedom', ch. 13 in his book *Liberal Rights: Collected Papers 1981–1991* (Cambridge University Press, Cambridge,1993), pp. 309–338.

12 To those who say that the streets and subway are not places for sleeping; that parks are not places for urinating or cooking, Waldron's response is this: perhaps they ought not to be; just as there ought not to be people who are without any place to call home. But it is only because those of us who are not homeless have somewhere else to eat, sleep and urinate that parks, streets and subways do not fulfil these purposes for us. 'The subway is a place where those who have some other place to sleep may do things besides sleeping.' For those who lack anywhere of their own, public space provides their only chances of meeting their basic needs legally and with some modicum of privacy.

13 Jonathan Wolff and Avner de-Shalit, *Disadvantage* (Oxford University Press, Oxford, 2007). The discussion of gratitude and reciprocity and care can be found at 45–46.

14 Iris Marion Young, *A Room of One's Own: Old Age, Extended Care, and Privacy*, in ed. Beate Rossler, *Privacies: Philosophical Evaluations* (Stanford University Press, Stanford, CA, 2004), pp. 168–169. The quotation is at 168.

Index

abortion 55
absolute monarchy 56
accountability 26, 28, 34, 45, 58
anonymity 3, 4, 5, 24, 71, 72, 78, 80
Apple 40
Aristotle 11
Ashe, Arthur 40–1
association, freedom of 4, 9, 61, 65, 76
Athenian democracy 8
autobiographies 42, 43, 44

Benn, Stanley 17, 38, 73
Bentham, Jeremy 14
Blair, Tony 39
Brandeis, Louis 35–6
Brennan, Geoffrey 25

Caen, Herb 31
Cambodia 66
celebrities 44, 95n
childbearing 53
childbirth 1, 55
children 43, 51, 52–3, 58, 59, 66, 67–8
China 66
choice, freedom of 4, 9, 61
citizenship, democratic 25–6
closed circuit television (CCTV) 74

Cohen, Joshua 54
Coke, Sir Edward 48
collective property 76–9, 82
collective responsibility 66–8, 71
confidentiality 3, 4, 5–6, 35, 37, 45, 61, 71–2, 76, 80
Conservative Party 39
constitutional democracy 59–60
control of personal information 1, 5, 6, 34

Dacre, Paul 89n
democracy 2, 3, 8–10, 17–29, 52, 61–2, 63, 64–5, 68 *see also* secret ballot
de-Shalit, Avner 80–1
diaries: privacy interests in 35–6
disadvantage: Wolff and de-Shalit's study of 80–1
discretion/tact 18, 35, 81
domestic affairs 4, 5, 6, 45, 47, 57, 59, 60, 63, 80
duty/duties 1, 5, 27, 28, 35, 49, 52, 59, 64–5, 67–8

election fraud 40
employee privacy 55–6
'employment at will' 55–6
'Englishman's home is his castle, An' 48–54, 60

equality 2, 4, 8, 11–12, 14, 24, 27, 28, 34, 40, 47, 50, 53, 57–8, 59, 60, 62, 63, 65, 71, 85
ethics of outing *see* outing
ethics of publicity *see* publication
exclusivity 6, 63
expression, freedom of 4, 9, 22, 24, 26, 27, 28–9, 37, 40–4, 61, 65, 76

facial recognition technologies 74
family/familial 5, 9, 45, 47–8, 51–3, 57, 58, 61, 62, 63, 64, 69–70
feminism 22–3
feudal societies 8, 48, 49, 50, 52, 53, 56, 60
Ford, President 31
freedom 2, 11–12, 14, 34, 35, 47, 48, 50, 57, 60, 63, 67, 85; of association 4, 9, 61, 65, 76; of choice 4, 9, 61; of expression 4, 9, 22, 24, 26, 27, 28–9, 40–4, 61, 65, 76; of the press 28, 29, 40–4; of religion 13; *see also* liberty

global positioning systems (GPS) 74
gossip, publication of 37, 38–9
Guardianship Act (1973) 52–3, 58–9

happiness 24, 50, 62, 65, 85, 86
home 48–54, 60, 74; privacy beyond the 54–62
homelessness 78–9
homosexuality 20
hypocrisy 6, 18, 33, 34, 39

immorality 25, 27, 39, 40 *see also* morality
information, personal 1, 3, 5, 18, 34–5, 94–5n

instrumental arguments 17–20, 24, 33, 62
intimacy 4, 54, 71, 80, 82
intrinsic arguments 17–18, 20–2, 41

Jobs, Steve 40
jury service 67

'kiss and tell' stories 42–3, 44

legal protection of rights 22–3
legal rights 12–15, 52, 59, 60
liberty 4, 7, 8, 11–12, 49, 60, 62, 75, 76 *see also* freedom

MacKinnon, Catherine 22–3
marriage 49–50, 61–3
maternal duties 68
Maynard, Joyce 4, 75–6
media 19–20, 43
military 48, 56–7, 67
Milk, Harvey 31, 32
Mill, John Stuart 22, 25, 37–8, 64–5
minorities 68, 83
MMR vaccination 39
Moore, Sara Jane 31
moral rights 4, 12–15, 41, 52, 60, 71–2, 73, 74, 82
morality 2, 17, 18, 21, 26, 34, 37, 39, 42, 45, 48, 53, 83 *see also* immorality

Nagel, Thomas 18, 19, 29
New York apartment blocks 77–8
North Korea 66
Nozick, Robert 11

open voting 25, 26–7
outing 3, 29, 31–4, 38–9

parents 58–9, 62, 66, 67–8
Parkinson, Cecil 39
personal information 1, 3, 5, 18, 34–5, 94–5n
personal responsibility 66–8
Pettit, Phillip 25
Plato 64
pregnancy 55
press: freedom of 28, 29, 40–4, 41
privacy: benefits of 85; defining and describing 3–5; different meanings of 5–8; international dimension 84; objections to 61–5, 69, 71–6, 85; political importance of 19; protection of 1, 3, 22–3, 28, 35–6, 37, 41, 42–3, 47, 52, 53, 54, 56, 57, 61, 63, 85; reasons to value 65; right to 3, 49, 63, 71–3, 74, 76, 82; as a social practice 21; synonyms for 5; value of 17–23, 85, 86
private property 77, 78, 79–82, 83
property 3, 71, 74, 75; collective 76–9, 82; private 77, 78, 79–82, 83; public 78, 80
property rights 69, 72–3, 75–6
property-like rights over our bodies 71, 72, 73, 74, 75
public shaming 26–7
public space/property 6, 78, 79, 80
public/private 57–8
publication: privacy and ethics of 34–9

Rachels, James 18
Reiman, Jeffrey 17, 20–1, 22
religion, freedom of 13
reproduction 3, 22, 47, 61

responsibility: personal and collective 66–8
right(s): legal 12–15, 52, 59, 60; moral 4, 12–15, 41, 52, 60, 71–2, 73, 74, 82; to marry 49–50; to privacy 3, 49, 63, 71–3, 74, 76, 82; to vote 14–15, 23–4

Salinger, J.D. 4, 75–6
San Francisco Chronicle 31
seclusion 4, 5, 6, 24, 57, 71
secret ballot 2, 10, 23–8, 29, 37
sex/sexual 6, 19, 43, 44, 47, 51, 53, 59, 63; privacy protection for 3, 54–5, 57, 61, 62, 64
sexual orientation: publication without consent *see* outing
shaming, public 26–7
Sipple, Oliver 31–3
slavery 11
small businesses 55
solitude 4, 71, 78, 82
Soviet Union 66
suicide 53

tact/discretion 18, 35, 81
Thatcher, Margaret 39
Thomson, Judith 7, 71–6, 82
Tocqueville, Alexis de 8, 64

United States 27, 41, 55–6, 67
utilitarians 14

Vicker, Joan 52
voting: open 25, 26–7; right to 14–15, 23–4; and secret ballot 2, 10, 23–8, 29, 37

Waldron, Jeremy 78–9
Wolff, Jonathan 80–1

women 55, 68, 85; legal guardianship of their children 52–3, 58–9; and legal views of privacy 22–3

Woolf, Virginia, *A Room of One's Own* 23
workplace, privacy protections 55–6

Young, Iris Marion 82

For Product Safety Concerns and Information please contact our EU
representative GPSR@taylorandfrancis.com
Taylor & Francis Verlag GmbH, Kaufingerstraße 24, 80331 München, Germany

www.ingramcontent.com/pod-product-compliance
Lightning Source LLC
Chambersburg PA
CBHW070303230426
43664CB00014B/2623